This edition copyright © Robert Frederick

Montague House, Lambridge Street, Bath BA1 6RX

First Published 1996

Acknowledgments

Design concept: Revue Design © Robert Frederick

Printed in Singapore by Star Standard Industries Pte. Ltd.

Whilst every care has been taken in compiling the information in this book, the publishers cannot accept responsibility
for any errors, inadvertent or not, that may be found, or may occur at some time in the future, for any reason.

The Really Useful Home Book

*A Compendium of Information, Handy Hints,
Planning Pages, Recipes and Quotations*

List of Contents

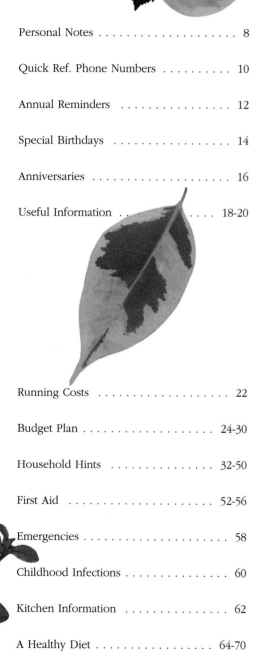

Name ....

Address ....

....

....

....

☎ Home ....

    Business .... Car ....

Social Security No: ....

Driving License No: ....

Vaccinations ....

....

In Case of Emergency notify ....

....

....

Accountant	Optician ....
Airport	Plumber ....
Bank	Railway Station ....
Saving Society	Solicitor ....
Club	Taxi/Car Hire ....
Dentist	Travel Agent ....
Doctor	Vet ....
Electrician	Water ....
Gas	Other ....

USEFUL INFORMATION

Bank Account No.	Car Key No. ....
Passport No.	Car Insurance Policy No. ....
Saving Society Account No.	Renewal Date ....
Credit Card No.s	Car Membership No. ....
Social Security No.	Driving Licence No. ....

Sonnet XLIII, from The Portuguese

How do I love thee?
   Let me count the ways.
I love thee to the depth and
   breadth and height
My soul can reach, when feeling
   out of sight,
For the ends of Being and ideal
   Grace.
I love thee to the level of every day's
Most quiet need, by sun and
   candlelight.
I love thee freely, as men strive
   for Right;
I love thee purely, as they turn
   from Praise.
I love thee with the passion
   put to use
In my old griefs, and with my
   childhood's faith.
I love thee with a love I seemed
   to lose
With my lost saints,—I love thee
   with the breath,
Smiles, tears, of all my life!—and,
   if God choose,
I shall but love thee better after
   death.

Elizabeth Barrett Browning

Name ....

Address ....

....

....

Tel ....

Name ....

Address ....

....

....

Tel ....

Name ....

Address ....

....

....

Tel ....

Name ....

Address ....

....

....

Tel ....

Name ....

Address ....

....

....

Tel ....

Telephone Numbers

Quick Reference

Name .... ☎ ....

Name .... ☎ ....

Name .... ☎ ....

Name .... ☎ ....

Name .... ☎ ....

Name .... ☎ ....

Name .... ☎ ....

Name .... ☎ ....

Name .... ☎ ....

Name .... ☎ ....

Name .... ☎ ....

Name .... ☎ ....

Name .... ☎ ....

Name .... ☎ ....

Name .... ☎ ....

Name .... ☎ ....

Name .... ☎ ....

Name .... ☎ ....

Name .... ☎ ....

Name .... ☎ ....

Thoughts for Everyday

"Our hours in love have wings; in absence crutches."

Colley Cibber

"Every baby born into the world is a finer one than the last."

Charles Dickens:
Nicholas Nickleby

"Those undeserved joys which come uncalled and make us more pleased than grateful are they that sing."

Thoreau

Name ....
Address ....
....
....
Tel ....

Name ....
Address ....
....
....
Tel ....

Name ....
Address ....
....
....
Tel ....

Name ....
Address ....
....
....
Tel ....

Name ....
Address ....
....
....
Tel ....

Annual Reminders

PERSONAL

Insurance - Life . . . .

    Health . . . .

    Savings Plans . . . .

Clubs/Societies . . . .

Subscriptions . . . .

Season Tickets . . . .

HOME

Insurance - Buildings . . . .

    Contents . . . .

TV/Cable . . . .

HP Payments/Loans . . . .

Mortgage/Rent . . . .

Local Taxes . . . .

Monthly/quarterly bills:

    Electricity . . . .

    Gas . . . .

    Telephone . . . .

    Water Bills . . . .

Standing Orders/DD . . . .

CAR

Tax . . . .

Insurance . . . .

Service . . . .

Vehicle Recovery . . . .

DETAILS/OTHER REMINDERS

Thoughts
for
Everyday

"The winds and waves are always on the side of the ablest navigators."

Edward Gibbon

"Gratitude is the heart's memory."

French Proverb

"Everyone is a genius at least once a year. The real geniuses simply have their bright ideas closer together."

George Christoph Lichtenberg

Name ....

Address ....

....

....

Tel ....

Name ....

Address ....

....

....

Tel ....

Name ....

Address ....

....

....

Tel ....

Name ....

Address ....

....

....

Tel ....

Name ....

Address ....

....

....

Tel ....

Special Birthdays

Spouse ....

Children ....

....

....

....

....

....

Grandchildren

....

....

....

....

....

....

....

....

Mother ....

Father ....

Mother-in-law ....

Father-in-law ....

Brothers & Sisters

....

....

....

....

....

....

Other Relations

....

....

....

....

....

....

....

Close Friends

....

....

....

....

....

....

....

....

....

Other

....

....

....

....

....

....

Thoughts for Everyday

"Genius is 1 per cent inspiration and 99 per cent perspiration."

Thomas A Edison

"An adventure is only an inconvenience rightly considered. An inconvenience is only an adventure wrongly considered."

G K Chesterton

"Many people lose their tempers merely from seeing you keep yours."

Frank Moore Colby

Name ....

Address ....

....

....

Tel ....

Name ....

Address ....

....

....

Tel ....

Name ....

Address ....

....

....

Tel ....

Name ....

Address ....

....

....

Tel ....

Name ....

Address ....

....

....

Tel ....

Anniversaries

Occasion ....   Date ....

Occasion ....   Date ....

Occasion ....   Date ....

Occasion ....   Date ....

Occasion ....   Date ....

Occasion ....   Date ....

Occasion ....   Date ....

Occasion ....   Date ....

Occasion ....   Date ....

Occasion ....   Date ....

Occasion ....   Date ....

Occasion ....   Date ....

~ WEDDING ANNIVERSARIES ~

First	Paper	Tenth	Tin	Thirtieth	Pearl
Second	Cotton	Eleventh	Steel	Thirty-fifth	Coral
Third	Leather	Twelfth	Silk, Linen	Forty-fifth	Sapphire
Fourth	Fruit, Flowers	Thirteenth	Lace	Fortieth	Ruby
Fifth	Wood	Fourteenth	Ivory	Fiftieth	Gold
Sixth	Sugar, Iron	Fifteenth	Crystal	Fifty-fifth	Emerald
Seventh	Wool, Copper	Twentieth	China	Sixtieth	Diamond
Eighth	Bronze, Pottery	Twenty-fifth	Silver	Seventieth	Platinum
Ninth	Pottery, Willow			Seventy-fifth	Diamond

METRIC CONVERSIONS	*multiply by*
acres to hectares	0.4047
cubic inches to cubic centimetres	16.39
cubic feet to cubic metres	0.02832
cubic yards to cubic metres	0.7646
cubic inches to litres	0.01639
feet to metres	0.3048
gallons to litres	4.546
grains to grammes	0.0648
inches to centimetres	2.540
miles to kilometres	1.609

METRIC CONVERSIONS	*multiply by*
ounces to grammes	28.35
pounds to kilogrammes	0.4536
pounds to grammes	453.6
square inches to square centimetres	6.452
square feet to square metres	0.0929
square yards to square metres	0.8361
square miles to square kilometres	2.590
tons to kilogrammes	1016.00
yards to metres	0.9144

LENGTH

1 centimetre (cm)	=	0.3937 in		
1 metre (m)	=	100 cm	=	1.0936 yds
1 kilometre (km)	=	1000 m	=	0,6214 mile
1 inch		2.5400 cm		
1 yard	=	36 in	=	0.9144 m
1 mile	=	1760 yds	=	1.6093 km

AREA

1 sq metre (m²)	=	10 000 cm²	=	1.1960 sq yds
1 hectare (ha)	=	10 000 m²	=	2.4711 acres
1 sq km (km²)	=	100 hectares	=	0.3861 sq mile
1 sq yd	=	9 sq ft	=	0.8361 m²
1 acre	=	4840 sq yds	=	4046.9 m²

CAPACITY

1 cu dm (dm³)	=	1000 cm³	=	0.0353 cu ft
1 cu metre (m³)	=	1000 dm³	=	1.3080 cu yds
1 litre	=	1 dm²	=	0.2200 gallon
1 cu yd	=	27 cu ft	=	0.7646 m³
1 pint	=	4 gills	=	0.5683 litre
1 gallon	=	8 pints	=	4.5461 litres

WEIGHT

1 gramme (g)	=	1000 mg	=	0.3535 oz
1 kilogramme (kg)	=	1000 g	=	2.2046 lb
1 tonne (t)	=	1000 kg	=	0.9842 ton
1 ounce	=	437.5 grains	=	28.350 g
1 pound	=	16 oz	=	0.4536 kg
1 ton	=	2240 pounds	=	1.0161 tonnes

A Red Red Rose

O my Luve's like a red, red rose,
That's newly sprung in June;
O my Luve's like the melodie
That's sweetly play'd in tune.

As fair art thou, my bonie lass,
So deep in luve am I;
And I will love thee still, my Dear,
Till a' the seas gang dry.

Till a' the seas gang dry, my Dear,
And the rocks melt wi' the sun:
I will love thee still, my Dear,
While the sands o' life shall run.

And fare thee weel, my only Luve!
And fare thee weel, a while!
And I will come again, my Luve,
Tho' it were ten thousand mile!

Robert Burns

To Electra

I dare not ask a kiss,
I dare not beg a smile,
Lest having that, or this,
I might grow proud the while.

No, no, the utmost share
Of my desire shall be,
Only to kiss the air,
That lately kissèd thee.

Robert Herrick

Name ....
Address ....
....
....
Tel ....

Name ....
Address ....
....
....
Tel ....

Name ....
Address ....
....
....
Tel ....

Name ....
Address ....
....
....
Tel ....

Name ....
Address ....
....
....
Tel ....

CLOTHING SIZES

Men's Suits & Overcoats

American	36	38	40	42	44	46
British	36	38	40	42	44	46
European	46	48	51	54	56	59

Women's Suits & Dresses

American	8	10	12	14	16	18
British	10	12	14	16	18	20
European	38	40	42	44	46	48

Shirts

American	14	14½	15	15½	16	16½	17
British	14	14½	15	15½	16	16½	17
European	36	37	38	39	41	42	43

Note: Size equivalents are approximate

ROMAN NUMERALS

I	=	1	XVI	=	16
II	=	2	XVII	=	17
III	=	3	XVIII	=	18
IV	=	4	XIX	=	19
V	=	5	XX	=	20
VI	=	6	XXX	=	30
VII	=	7	XL	=	40
VIII	=	8	L	=	50
IX	=	9	LX	=	60
X	=	10	LXX	=	70
XI	=	11	LXXX	=	80
XII	=	12	XC	=	90
XIII	=	13	C	=	100
XIV	=	14	D	=	500
XV	=	15	M	=	1000

INTERNATIONAL PAPER SIZES (A SERIES)

SIZE	MILLIMETRES			INCHES		
A0	841	x	1189	33.1	x	46.8
A1	594	x	841	23.4	x	33.1
A2	420	x	594	16.5	x	23.4
A3	297	x	420	11.7	x	16.5
A4	210	x	297	8.3	x	11.7
A5	148	x	210	5.8	x	8.3
A6	105	x	148	4.1	x	5.8
A7	74	x	105	2.9	x	4.1

CLOTHING SIZES

Men's Shoes

American	7½	8	8½	9½	10½	11½
British	7	7½	8	9	10	11
European	40½	41	42	43	44½	46

Women's Shoes

American	6	6½	7	7½	8	8½
British	4½	5	5½	6	6½	7
European	37½	38	39	39½	40	40½

Children's Clothes

American	4	6	8	10	12	14
British [Height (in)]	43	48	55	58	60	62
European [Height (in)]	109	122	140	147	152	57

Note: Size equivalents are approximate

WIND SPEEDS

1	7 mph light wind
2	11 mph light breeze
3	16 mph gentle breeze
4	20 mph moderate breeze
5	25 mph fresh breeze
6	30 mph strong breeze
7	35 mph moderate gale
8	45 mph fresh gale
9	50 mph strong gale
10	60 mph whole gale
11	70 mph storm
12	80 mph hurricane

TEMPERATURE

F'heit	22°F	32°F	41°F	59°F	68°F	86°F
Celsius	-5°C	0°C	5°C	15°C	20°C	30°C

Conversion Formulae

$$C = \frac{5}{9}(F - 32)$$
$$F = \frac{9}{5}(C + 32)$$

Thoughts for Everyday

"A diamond is a chunk of coal that made good under pressure."

Anon

"The great mind knows the power of gentleness, Only tries force because persuasion fails."

Robert Browning

"Animals are such agreeable friends – they ask no questions, they pass no criticisms."

George Eliot

Name ....

Address ....

....

....

Tel ....

Name ....

Address ....

....

....

Tel ....

Name ....

Address ....

....

....

Tel ....

Name ....

Address ....

....

....

Tel ....

Name ....

Address ....

....

....

Tel ....

C

RUNNING COSTS OF DOMESTIC GAS APPLIANCES

Gas is sold by the therm. The price you pay for one therm can be found on your gas bill.

The rate at which different appliances burn gas varies, so the figures quoted are average.

Cooker   Grill .... 7 hours on full
             Hotplate................... 9 hours of full
             Oven .... 36 hours on Gas Mark 2
             .... 26 hours on Gas Mark 5
Gas Fire .... 5 hours on high setting
             .... 10 hours on low setting

RUNNING COSTS OF DOMESTIC ELECTRICAL APPLIANCES

Electricity is sold by the unit. One unit is consumed by using electricity continuously at the rate of one kilowatt (1000 watts) for one hour. This means for example, that for one unit a 100W bulb will burn continuously for 10 hours, a 250W appliance will run for 4 hours and a 1Kw (kilowatt) fire will operate for 1 hour.

The price you pay for each unit can be found on your electricity bill or you can obtain details of available tariffs including any lower cost night rates, from your Electricity Board.

LARGER APPLIANCES

Cooker
One week's meals for a family of 4 .... 17 units
Dishwasher (Full load).......................... 2 units
Fridge Freezer .... About 2 units a day
Freezer (upright) .... 1-2 units a day
Washing Machine (automatic)
    Weekly wash* for family of 4 .... 5 units
Washing Machine (twin-tub)
    Weekly wash* for family of 4 .... 12 units

(*17 kg or 37 lb dry weight of laundry)

WHAT YOU GET FOR ONE UNIT FROM TYPICAL DOMESTIC APPLIANCES

Carving Knife .... approx 220 joints
Coffee Percolator .... 75 cups of coffee
Contact Grill .... 25 medium steaks
2Kw Convector Heater .... 1/2 hour
Extractor Fan .... 24 hours
2Kw Fan Heater .... 1/2 hour
Infra-Red Heater .... 1 hour
Iron (hand) .... over 2 hours
Kettle .... 12 pints of water
Light (100W lamp or 1,500mm (5ft)
    fluorescent tube) .... 10 hours
700W Microwave Heater........ 8 chicken pieces
3Kw Radiant Heater .... 20 minutes
Radio .... 20 hours
Record Player .... over 24 hours
Refrigerator (compressor type) .... 1 day
Spin Dryer .... about 5 weeks' laundry
Stereo System .... 8-10 hours
Tape Recorder .... over 24 hours
Tea Maker .... 35 cups of tea
Television (colour) .... 12 hours
Tumble Dryer .... approx 1/2 hour
Vacuum Cleaner .... 2-4 hours

Thoughts for Everyday

"They are able because they think they are able."

Virgil

"Winning is not a sometime thing; it's an all-time thing. You don't win once in a while, you don't do things right once in a while, you do them right all the time. Winning is a habit. Unfortunately, so is losing."

Vince Lombardi

"The only way to get the best of an argument is to avoid it."

Dale Carnegie

Name ....

Address ....

....

....

Tel ....

Name ....

Address ....

....

....

Tel ....

Name ....

Address ....

....

....

Tel ....

Name ....

Address ....

....

....

Tel ....

Name ....

Address ....

....

....

Tel ....

Budget Planner

EXPENDITURE	Jan	Feb	Mar	INCOME	Jan	Feb	Mar
Mortgage/Rent				Salary A			
Local Taxes				Salary B			
Bills – Gas				Bonus			
Bills – Electricity				Dividends			
Bills – Telephone				Interest			
Bills – Water				Pension/Savings			
Insurance Polices				Other			
Pension/Savings Plans				Other			
Credit Card Charges				Other			
Loans				Total			
Groceries – Food							
Groceries – Other							
Travel/Car							
Holidays							
Leisure/Entertainment							
Gifts							
Personal							
Clothes							
Household Expenses							
Other							
Other							
Other							
Other							
Total							

January

Income Total	....
Expenditure Total	....
Balance	....

February

Income Total	....
Expenditure Total	....
Balance	....

March

Income Total	....
Expenditure Total	....
Balance	....

Thoughts for Everyday

"Sometimes when one person is missing, the whole world seems depopulated."

Lamartine

"Don't let what you cannot do interfere with what you can do."

John Wooden

"You will always find some Eskimos ready to instruct the Congolese on how to cope with heat waves."

Stanislaw Lec

Name ....
Address ....
....
....
Tel ....

Name ....
Address ....
....
....
Tel ....

Name ....
Address ....
....
....
Tel ....

Name ....
Address ....
....
....
Tel ....

Name ....
Address ....
....
....
Tel ....

Budget Planner

EXPENDITURE	Apr	May	Jun
Mortgage/Rent			
Local Taxes			
Bills – Gas			
Bills – Electricity			
Bills – Telephone			
Bills – Water			
Insurance Polices			
Pension/Savings Plans			
Credit Card Charges			
Loans			
Groceries – Food			
Groceries – Other			
Travel/Car			
Holidays			
Leisure/Entertainment			
Gifts			
Personal			
Clothes			
Household Expenses			
Other			
Other			
Other			
Other			
Total			

INCOME	Apr	May	Jun
Salary A			
Salary B			
Bonus			
Dividends			
Interest			
Pension/Savings			
Other			
Other			
Other			
Total			

April
Income Total	....
Expenditure Total	....
Balance	....

May
Income Total	....
Expenditure Total	....
Balance	....

June
Income Total	....
Expenditure Total	....
Balance	....

Budget Planner

EXPENDITURE	Jul	Aug	Sep	INCOME	Jul	Aug	Sep
Mortgage/Rent				Salary A			
Local Taxes				Salary B			
Bills – Gas				Bonus			
Bills – Electricity				Dividends			
Bills – Telephone				Interest			
Bills – Water				Pension/Savings			
Insurance Polices				Other			
Pension/Savings Plans				Other			
Credit Card Charges				Other			
Loans				Total			
Groceries – Food							
Groceries – Other							
Travel/Car							
Holidays							
Leisure/Entertainment							
Gifts							
Personal							
Clothes							
Household Expenses							
Other							
Other							
Other							
Other							
Total							

July
Income Total ....

Expenditure Total ....

Balance ....

August
Income Total ....

Expenditure Total ....

Balance ....

September
Income Total ....

Expenditure Total ....

Balance ....

No Loathsomeness in Love

What I fancy, I approve,
No dislike there is in love:
Be my Mistress short or tall,
And distorted therewithal:
Be she likewise one of those,
That an acre hath of nose:
Be her forehead, and her eyes
Full of incongruities:
Be her cheeks so shallow too,
As to shew her tongue wag
    through:
Be her lips ill hung, or set,
And her grinders black as jet;
Has she thin hair, hath she none,
She's to me a paragon.

Robert Herrick

from Prometheus Unbound

All love is sweet,
Given or returned. Common as
    light is love,
And its familiar voice wearies
    not ever. . . .
Those who inspire it most
    are fortunate,
As I am now; but those who
    feel it most
Are happier still.

Percy Bysshe Shelley

E

Name ....
Address ....
....
....
Tel ....

Name ....
Address ....
....
....
Tel ....

Name ....
Address ....
....
....
Tel ....

Name ....
Address ....
....
....
Tel ....

Name ....
Address ....
....
....
Tel ....

Budget Planner

EXPENDITURE	Oct	Nov	Dec	INCOME	Oct	Nov	Dec
Mortgage/Rent				Salary A			
Local Taxes				Salary B			
Bills – Gas				Bonus			
Bills – Electricity				Dividends			
Bills – Telephone				Interest			
Bills – Water				Pension/Savings			
Insurance Polices				Other			
Pension/Savings Plans				Other			
Credit Card Charges				Other			
Loans				Total			
Groceries – Food							
Groceries – Other							
Travel/Car							
Holidays							
Leisure/Entertainment							
Gifts							
Personal							
Clothes							
Household Expenses							
Other							
Other							
Other							
Other							
Total							

October

Income Total ....

Expenditure Total ....

Balance ....

November

Income Total ....

Expenditure Total ....

Balance ....

December

Income Total ....

Expenditure Total ....

Balance ....

Thoughts for Everyday

"He who builds to every man's advice will have a crooked house."

Danish Proverb

"Aim at the sun, and you may not reach it; but your arrow will fly far higher than if aimed at an object on a level with yourself."

J Hawes

"Of cheerfulness, or a good temper – the more it is spent, the more of it remains."

Ralph Waldo Emerson

Name ....

Address ....

....

....

Tel ....

Name ....

Address ....

....

....

Tel ....

Name ....

Address ....

....

....

Tel ....

Name ....

Address ....

....

....

Tel ....

Name ....

Address ....

....

....

Tel ....

ANIMAL HAIR

Use sellotape to remove animal hair from clothes, furniture etc. Simply wrap the sellotape around your fingers (sticky side outward) and rub over the hairs.

ANTS

You can discourage ants in the house by sprinkling bicarbonate of soda or powdered borax of cloves on shelves and in drawers.

ASH

Do not empty these into a wastepaper basket as they can easily start a fire. A large tin is much more suitable. To prevent cigarette ends from burning in an ashtray and to reduce the smell of stale tobacco, coat the bottom of the ashtray with baking powder.

BAKING TINS

To discourage a new baking tin from rusting, rub it inside and out with lard and place it in an oven at moderate heat for forty-five minutes. When cool wipe thoroughly with a paper towel. To remove rust from tinware rub with half a raw potato that has been dipped in scouring powder. Rinse and then dry - ideally in an oven.

BALL POINT PENS

If a ballpoint pen doesn't work try warming the point gently with a match or by pouring boiling water over it.

BARBECUE

To maximise the heat line your barbecue with tin-foil, shiny side up. Use left over brewed coffee to clean the barbecue set.

BATHS

If you have unsightly stains on your bath or wash basin due to a dripping tap, try rubbing with a paste made of lemon juice and salt and rinsing well. Failing this, try rubbing them with a toothbrush using a paste of cream of tartar and peroxide and then rinsing.

BOOKS

To keep your books in good condition do not place them tight against a wall, but leave a couple of centimetres gap to enable the air to circulate around them. Also, make sure they are kept upright and not leaning at an angle as this would be bad for their bindings.

If the pages of a book are torn slightly, place them in position and smear lightly with the white of an egg, leaving the book open to dry.

Carpet tape is useful when trying to repair the spine of a book.

BOTTLES

Stick an adhesive plaster over the cork of the bottle containing liquid when packing to help prevent accidents. It is also advisable to pack bottles between soft items.

Bottles are best emptied by shaking them in a circular motion.

If you find difficulty unscrewing a bottle or container give a firm tap to the bottom of the container.

Remove strong odours from bottles by filling them with a mixture of cold water and four teaspoons of dry mustard and leaving them to stand for a least half a day before rinsing well.

BREAD BOARDS

If your wooden bread board is warped, place it on a flat surface and cover it with a wet cloth, leaving it for at least 24 hours.

Thoughts
for
Everyday

F

"Behold the turtle.
He makes progress only when
he sticks his neck out."

James B Conant

"He that is slow to anger is
better than 'he mighty; and
he that ruleth his spirit than
he that taketh a city."

Proverbs 16:32

"To forget one's ancestors is to
be a brook without a source,
a tree without a root."

Chinese Proverb

Name ....

Address ....

....

....

Tel ....

Name ....

Address ....

....

....

Tel ....

Name ....

Address ....

....

....

Tel ....

Name ....

Address ....

....

....

Tel ....

Name ....

Address ....

....

....

Tel ....

BROOMS

When a broom handle does not fit anymore then wrap with adhesive tape and screw the handle back into the socket. This should help to keep it in place.

CANDLES

To increase the life span of candles keep them in the freezer for a few hours before use.

To make candles fit into candle sticks dip the end in hot water until it is soft enough to fit into the required size.

Wash the candle stick holder in soapy water with a few drops of ammonia to remove the wax.

CAR

To prevent bumping your car in a tight garage attach an old tyre to the wall.

To clean a very dirty car use a mixture of methylated spirit and water (1 unit of methylated spirit to 8 units of water). Do not rinse. This should leave your car shining.

CARPETS

When choosing a carpet ask to see it flat on the floor. The colour might look quite different when the carpet is displayed rolled vertically.

To restore the life to carpet pile which has been flattened by furniture legs, place several layers of wet cloth onto the area. Then hold a hot iron lightly on top of the cloth. The steam should bring back the bounce to the carpet which can then be fluffed up using a nail brush.

CHINA

Protect your best china plates from chips and cracks by alternating them with paper plates or corrugated paper when storing them or when packing them.

COOKING SMELLS

Get rid of unwanted cooking smells by boiling one teaspoon of ground cinnamon or ground cloves in a 1/4 litre of water for fifteen minutes.

CORK

Cork expands. If it does not fit back into the bottle then place it in boiling water for a few minutes until it becomes soft. It will then fit easily back into the bottle.

CRYSTAL

To give a real sparkle to your crystal add a few drops of ammonia to the washing water and vinegar to the rinsing water.

DAMPNESS

To determine whether dampness is caused by condensation or is coming from outside, attach a piece of silver foil to the affected area. If moisture appears on the front surface then this is caused by condensation in the room and you should look for better ways of ventilating the room. If, however, the foil is wet on the side of the wall, the damp comes from the outside and you should seek professional help.

DECORATING

When you have decorated a room, make sure you keep a note of the number of rolls of wallpaper or tins of paint that you used, so that when you come to redecorating, you will know exactly what you need.

DISHWASHERS

Pour 4 heaped tablespoons of bicarbonate of soda through the bottom rack of your dishwasher and put it on the rinse cycle to refresh the smell.

Thoughts for Everyday

"Challenges can be stepping stones or stumbling blocks. It's just a matter of how you view them."

Author Unidentified

"To travel hopefully is better than to arrive."

Sir James Jeans

"I am only one; but still I am one. I cannot do everything, but still I can do something; I will not refuse to do something I can do."

Hellen Keller

Name ....

Address ....

....

....

Tel ....

Name ....

Address ....

....

....

Tel ....

Name ....

Address ....

....

....

Tel ....

Name ....

Address ....

....

....

Tel ....

Name ....

Address ....

....

....

Tel ....

DOORS

Silence a creaky door by rubbing soap along the hinges.

DRAWERS

If you have trouble opening tight fitting drawers, rub soap or candle wax along the upper edges to lubricate them.

DRILLING

To stop the drill from slipping when drilling a hole into metal or ceramic tiles, cover the mark with adhesive tape, drill through it and then remove the tape.

When drilling into the ceiling, drill through the base of an old squash bottle or transparent plastic container and this will catch the chips and stop them from going into your eyes.

EASTER EGGS

Use natural products to dye Easter eggs: beetroot juice will make a red dye, saffron will give you yellow, and use spinach juice for a green colour.

EGG BOXES

Cardboard or fibre egg boxes are ideal for growing seeds. When the shoots are ready for planting, just bury the entire tray. The roots will not be disturbed and the tray will disintegrate after a while.

ELECTRIC-WIRE

When fitting a plug it is often difficult to cut the rubber which encompasses the wire without cutting the copper thread. If you warm the rubber with a match you will be able to strip it very easily with your fingers.

ENAMEL

If your enamel is cracked and the cracks become dirty, make a thick paste of French chalk and water and coat the enamel with it. Leave it until the paste dries out and begins to crack and then brush off. Repeat until the cracks come clean.

ERASERS

Washing-up liquid effectively cleans dirty erasers.

FELT-TIPPED PENS

If your felt-tip pen seems to have run out, try dipping the tip in a little vinegar - this should give it a new lease of life. Store felt-tip pens tip downwards with the cap on so that they are always ready to use.

FINGER NAILS

If you want to take care of your nails, never cut them with scissors as this can cause them to split. File them with an emery board - from the sides up to the tip (and never in a see-saw movement) - as this is softer than a metal file.

FIREPLACES

If you are lighting a fire in a chimney which has not been used for some time and which may be damp, first burn a creased sheet of newspaper in the grate. This should remove the moisture from the chimney and help you get the best out of the fireplace. Do not burn coloured magazines or newspaper as the coloured ink will give off some lead vapour when burning.

FLIES

Basil or mint grown in pots on the windowsill or in a window box is a sweet smelling way of deterring flies.

FLOORS

Talcum powder sprinkled between floorboards will help to stop them from squeaking.

FLOWERS

If you are picking flowers from the garden, do not do it during the warmest part of the day as the flowers will not last long. Pick them in the early morning or early evening if you want them to last longer.

FOIL

Wrap food tightly in kitchen foil for storing but loosely for cooking.

FRAMING

Insert kitchen foil behind the picture when framing to prevent damage from damp.

FREEZER

When you have defrosted your freezer rub the inside with glycerine. Next time you come to defrost it you should find that the ice will come away easily.

To stop packages from sticking to the freezer walls or bottom, do not put them straight back into the freezer after defrosting but leave the freezer empty for half an hour first.

FURNITURE

When it is exposed to direct sunlight, polished furniture will permanently lose its veneer. To avoid lasting damage, either position the piece of furniture elsewhere, or keep it covered with a cloth.

FUSES

Keep a torch and a card of fuse wire beside the fuse box in case of an emergency.

GARLIC

To remove the smell of garlic from your breath chew some fresh mint, a coffee bean, a stalk of parsley or celery or some cardamom seeds!

GIFT WRAP

When you are wrapping large numbers of presents, at Christmas for example or at a children's party, try using attractive leftover wallpaper which makes a far cheaper alternative to gift wrap.

GLASSES

If two glasses have stuck together and you are finding it difficult to separate them, stand the bottom glass in hot (not boiling) water and fill the top one with cold water. This should cause them to separate without damaging them.

To get rid of small chips around the rim of a glass, rub them with fine sandpaper until smooth. Stand a silver spoon in a glass or jar to prevent it from cracking when boiling water is poured into it.

GLUE

Fit a piece of candle on the top of a glue bottle and use it as a stopper to close the bottle. As glue does not stick to candle wax you should no longer have any problems when you come to open it.

GRASS

To prevent grass from growing between the cracks in your paving stones or path, sprinkle salt in them, or pour on very salted boiling water.

GREENFLY

You can help to discourage greenfly by planting garlic around the plants that attract the greenfly. When the garlic starts sprouting, keep the shoots cut back.

Heart, We Will Forget Him

Heart, we will forget him!
You and I, tonight!
You may forget the warmth he gave,
I will forget the light.

When you have done, pray tell me,
That I may straight begin!
Haste! lest while you're lagging,
I may remember him!

Emily Dickinson

Love's Philosophy

The fountains mingle with the river .
And the rivers with the Ocean,
The winds of Heaven mix for ever
With a sweet emotion;
Nothing in the world is single;
All things by a law divine
In one spirit meet and mingle.
Why not I with thine?

See the mountains kiss high Heaven
And the waves clasp one another;
No sister-flower would be forgiven
If it disdained its brother;
And the sunlight clasps the earth
And the moonbeams kiss the sea:
What is all this sweet work worth
If thou kiss not me?

Percy Bysshe Shelley

Name ....

Address ....

....

....

Tel ....

Name ....

Address ....

....

....

Tel ....

Name ....

Address ....

....

....

Tel ....

Name ....

Address ....

....

....

Tel ....

Name ....

Address ....

....

....

Tel . ....

G

GUTTERS

A piece of chicken wire placed over the top of your gutter will effectively prevent falling leaves from blocking it.

HANGERS

If you have a skirt without any loops and are short of special hangers, wind a rubber band around each end of an ordinary hanger to prevent the skirt from falling off, or put two clothes pegs on an ordinary wire hanger.

HARD WATER DEPOSITS

If you find hard water deposits in jugs, bottles, vases or glasses etc., fill the object with malt vinegar and leave it for a few hours or as long as necessary. Then rub off with a fine wire scouring pad and rinse thoroughly. The vinegar can be reused.

HOSE

To make the hose fit easily onto the tap rub the inside of the hose with some soap. The soap will quickly dry when the hose is fitted.

HOT-WATER BOTTLES

When filling a hot-water bottle lie it flat on its back holding the neck upright. This will prevent the water splashing due to air-bubbles in the bottle. Add a little salt to the water to keep it warm longer.

INSECTS

By hanging a fresh bunch of stinging nettles in front of any open windows or doors, you can discourage flies and wasps from invading your house.

IRONING

Starch can be removed from the bottom of your iron by sprinkling a piece of paper with some fine kitchen salt and rubbing the iron over it until the base becomes smooth again, or by rubbing the base with half a lemon dipped in fine kitchen salt. A few drops of your favourite toilet water mixed with the water in the iron or sprinkled first on the ironing board will perfume your linen lightly.

IVORY

Very dirty ivory can be cleaned by leaving the item to soak for a few hours in milk and then washing it with warm soapy water. To keep small pieces of ivory white, place them in the direct sunlight. Alternatively, to colour a piece of ivory which looks too new, dip it in strong tea or coffee. Do not leave it to soak but keep dipping it in and out until the desired effect is reached. Dry and polish.

JARS

Leave a few drops of bleach in a glass jar to remove strong fish or pickle smells. You will have to leave the bleach in for at least twelve hours.

If you make some small holes in the lid of a jam jar or other glass screw-topped jar with a nail or skewer, you can use it as a cheap flour dredger or as a water sprinkler when ironing.

JAR LABELS

Do not label your jars until the contents have cooled, otherwise the labels will come unstuck.

Thoughts for Everyday

"If you don't stand for something, you'll fall for anything."

Author Unidentified

"When the One Great Scorer comes to write against your name, He marks, not that you won or lost, but how you played the game."

Grantland Rice

"A good natured man has the whole world to be happy out of."

Alexander Pope

Name ....
Address ....
....
....
Tel ....

Name ....
Address ....
....
....
Tel ....

Name ....
Address ....
....
....
Tel ....

Name ....
Address ....
....
....
Tel ....

Name ....
Address ....
....
....
Tel ....

G

JEWELLERY

If you want to give a quick shine to gold jewellery, rub the item with a ball of soft bread. Likewise if you want an item of silver jewellery to shine, rub it with half a lemon and then rinse before drying.

To loosen or remove a ring which is stuck on your finger, wash your hands with soap and water and try to take the ring off while the soap is still on your hands.

KETTLES

Place a marble in your kettle to prevent it from furring. To defur a kettle fill it with water and put the kettle in your freezer. When it defrosts the ice will pull the fur of the sides. Alternatively, pour in a small quantity of vinegar (enough to cover the element where applicable), bring it to the boil then agitate it. Leave it to cool and then rinse thoroughly. It may be necessary to repeat these processes several times.

KEYS

Covering a rusty key with turpentine and leaving it to soak for a couple of hours before rubbing and drying it should bring its shine back.

KNITWEAR

To prevent your knitwear from stretching when you are washing it in the washing machine, place it first inside a pillowcase.

LEATHER SHOES

When drying leather shoes or boots, never do so quickly in front of the fire as the leather will harden and will be more likely to crack.

LIDS

If you cannot unscrew a lid, place the jar in boiling water for a few minutes. It should then become loose and easy to unscrew.

LIGHT BULBS

You can delicately scent your room by rubbing just a few drops of your favourite perfume onto a light bulb. A pleasant smell will be emitted when the light bulb is on.

LINEN

To prevent fine linen which is not in constant use from becoming discoloured and yellow, wrap it in blue tissue paper.

LINOLEUM

Unsightly black marks on linoleum floors can be removed quite simply by using a pencil-eraser. A few drops of paraffin in the water when washing will help make linoleum shine.

LIPSTICK

When you are testing a lipstick for colour, the best place to try it is on the cushion of your finger, where the skin is pinkish, like the lips.

LOCKS

When you cannot get your key to turn in a lock and it seems to be jammed, rub the key with vaseline, or, failing that, butter or margarine. Alternatively, rub a key all over with pencil lead and work it in the lock several times. This will help to keep the lock in good working order.

MATCHES

A damp match can be made to light by coating the tip in nail varnish. You do not even have to wait for it to dry before striking it. An alternative is to rub it against the bristles of a brush.

Thoughts for Everyday

"When a man's stomach is full it makes no difference whether he is rich or poor."

Euripides: Electra

"I do not care to belong to a club that accepts people like me as members."

Groucho Marx

"A baby is an angel whose wings decrease as his legs increase."

French Proverb

Name ....

Address ....

....

....

Tel ....

Name ....

Address ....

....

....

Tel ....

Name ....

Address ....

....

....

Tel ....

Name ....

Address ....

....

....

Tel ....

Name ....

Address ....

....

....

Tel ....

H

MICROWAVE OVENS

You can help to remove stubborn and unpleasant cooking smells from inside a microwave oven by placing a teacup containing 3 parts water to 1 part lemon juice or vinegar inside it and cooking for eight to ten minutes on the lowest setting. Wipe the oven dry afterwards.

MIRRORS

If, before you run your bath, you rub the bathroom mirror with a few drops of shampoo, this will help prevent it from steaming up.

MOTHS

Small muslin bags filled with aromatic plants placed in your wardrobe and drawers will deter moths and will make your clothes smell nice at the same time.

NAILS

When hammering small nails use a hairslide as a holder or stick plasticine over the area you wish to hammer the nail into. This will hold the nail in position and will protect your fingers.

To prevent cracking the plaster when hammering in nails, first stick a piece of sellotape or masking tape to the wall, then hammer the nail in through the tape.

When trying to remove a nail which has been painted over, first soften the paint by holding a lighted match just below it, being careful not to burn the wall.

NAIL VARNISH

You can keep the top of a bottle of nail varnish from sticking and becoming difficult to open by spreading a little vaseline on the grooves.

Storing the bottle in the fridge will prevent the nail varnish from getting a sticky consistency and it will also help the varnish to last longer.

If the varnish thickens, it can be brought back to a better consistency by adding just a few drops of nail varnish remover.

NEWSPAPER

Roll a newspaper into a long thin tube, knotted in the middle, when you are lighting a fire.

OVENS

Next time you clean your oven, after cleaning and drying it rub it all over with a paste made of bicarbonate of soda and water. This should make it easier to wipe clean next time around.

PAINT

When selecting a single colour for the walls of a room, always choose one a shade lighter than you want, as paint tends to look darker once it is on the wall.

To keep the top of a paint tin clean, when painting place a paper plate over the top of the tin with the middle cut out. This way all the drops will land on the plate and not on the tin, and the plate can simply be discarded after you have finished painting.

The strong smell left in your house after you have been painting can be avoided by using a mixture of one tablespoon of vanilla essence to two pints paint when you are painting. Or while painting, try adding a couple of tablespoons of ammonia to one or two shallow containers of water placed in the room you are working on - this should stop the smell from spreading around the house.

Thoughts for Everyday

"The height of cleverness is to be able to conceal it."

François de la Rochefoucauld

"I keep my friends as misers do their treasure, because, of all the things granted us by wisdom, none is greater or better than friendship."

Pietro Aretino

"Content makes poor men rich; discontent makes rich men poor."

Benjamin Franklin

Name ....
Address ....
....
....
Tel ....

Name ....
Address ....
....
....
Tel ....

Name ....
Address ....
....
....
Tel ....

Name ....
Address ....
....
....
Tel ....

Name ....
Address ....
....
....
Tel ....

PAINTBRUSHES

Dried out brushes can be restored to life by immersing them in hot vinegar, while errant bristles can be encouraged to return to their proper place by spraying the brush head with hairspray, smoothing and leaving to dry.

PAINT TUBES

To get a stubborn cap off a small tube of artist's paint, try holding a lighted match under the cap for just a few seconds.

PAN

Before using a new pan, boil some vinegar in it for a few minutes to prevent food from sticking.

PARCELS

When wrapping a parcel using string, first dip the string in warm water and then tie the knot. When the string dries it will shrink, leaving a tight knot.

PIANOS

Do not place a lot of books or ornaments on the top of a piano as it will deaden the tone. If a piano key stays down when it is struck then it is a sign of dampness.

Ivory keys will become yellowed more quickly if the lid of the piano is kept down, as ivory yellows more in the dark.

PINS

Keep a small magnet in your pin box, then if you drop it the keys will be more likely to cluster around the magnet, making them easier to collect.

PLASTIC BOTTLES

For easier and more compact disposal of your plastic bottles, pour a small quantity of boiling water into the bottle. This will cause it to become soft and to collapse, making it easier to crush the bottle in your hands.

PLASTICINE

A quick and cheap substitute for plasticine for children to play with can be made by making a dough with flour, water and salt. This can be coloured with a little paprika or mustard powder, and will stay soft if stored in a sealed plastic bag. If you do not want to use a trellis but wish your ivy to grow up the wall, encourage it by sticking it to the wall from time to time with plasticine.

PLASTERS

If you find removing sticking plaster from your skin painful, first rub baby oil over the plaster. It should be easier to remove.

REFRIGERATORS

A piece of charcoal placed inside your fridge will absorb the smells of strong food such as fish and cheese and will only need replacing every 5-to-6 months.
If your fridge is noisy it could simply be that it is not standing on a level surface.

RUBBER GLOVES

Avoid hands sweating in rubber gloves by dusting the inside of the gloves with talc when you use them and by washing the insides from time to time. It will also help if you dry the gloves inside out after you have used them.

RUBBISH

To keep dogs and cats away from your rubbish sprinkle pure ammonia over the bags.

RUGS

To keep a rug from slipping or wrinkling on a carpet or shiny floor, stick some plastic stick-on it, commonly used for the bath, on the underside of the rug. Alternatively, you could sew or glue pieces of carpet, pile downwards, under the corners of the rug.

RUST

Rust on utensils can be removed by rubbing the stains with a cork dipped in olive oil. Rust stains on metal will sometimes disappear when rubbed with half a raw onion.

SHINE

Black or dark coloured clothes can become shiny with wear. Alleviated this by brushing the shiny part with black coffee – half a teacup of strong black coffee to half a teacup of water. Then press with a cloth. Alternatively, rub the article with a clean cloth dampened with turpentine or white spirit. The smell will soon disappear.

SHOES

When buying shoes, wait until the afternoon. Your feet tend to be relaxed first thing in the morning after a night's sleep but may swell slightly during the day, so if you buy shoes early in the morning you may find they pinch you in the evening.

Remove the odour from shoes by sprinkling a tablespoon of bicarbonate of soda inside each shoe and leaving it overnight.

When drying wet shoes, stuff with newspaper to help them keep their shape.

SHOWER CURTAINS

To prevent mildew on your cloth shower curtains, soak them for half an hour in a strong solution of salted water, then hang them up to dry.

Rubbing the curtains with bicarbonate of soda will also help remove mildew.

SLUGS

One of the less offensive ways of killing slugs is by distributing bran around the garden, which they are attracted to but which kills them. (The bran will also attract snails, who will assemble around it making it easy to collect them). Alternatively, you can entice the slugs with a glass of beer left in the garden overnight.

SMOKE

To prevent a room from becoming smoky when people are smoking in it, try lighting a few candles, or strategically arrange a few small containers filled with vinegar. This should help to eliminate the smoke from the room.

STAINS

When removing a stain, work from the edge of the stain inwards. This will help prevent the stain from spreading.

STAMPS

To remove an unused stamp from an envelope without damaging it, submerge the corner of the envelope with the stamp on it in boiling water for a few minutes. The stamp should then come off easily and can be left to dry. Another method is to wet the back of the stamp inside the envelope with lighter fluid.

STICKY LABELS

Stubborn sticky labels on glass or china can be removed with nail-varnish remover, cooking oil, turpentine or white spirit.

Untitled

If grief for grief can touch thee,
If answering woe for woe,
If any ruth can melt thee,
Come to me now!

I cannot be more lonely,
More drear I cannot be!
My worn heart throbs so wildly
'Twill break for thee.

And when the world despises,
When heaven repels my prayer,
Will not mine angel comfort?
Mine idol hear?

Yes, by the tears I've poured thee,
By all my hours of pain,
O I shall surely win thee,
Beloved, again!

Emily Bronte

In a Bath Teashop

'Let us not speak, for the love we
    bear one another—
Let us hold hands and look.'
She, such a very ordinary little
    woman;
He, such a thumping crook:
But both, for the moment, little
    lower than the angels
In the teashop inglenook.

John Betjeman

Name ....

Address ....

....

....

Tel ....

Name ....

Address ....

....

....

Tel ....

Name ....

Address ....

....

....

Tel ....

Name ....

Address ....

....

....

Tel ....

Name ....

Address ....

....

....

Tel ....

I

THERMOS FLASKS

To clean a stained thermos flask add three table-spoons of bicarbonate of soda and fill up with warm water. Agitate it and leave to stand for quarter of an hour. Then rinse and leave to dry. Stubborn coffee smells and stains can be eliminated by pouring in a cup of boiling water and one tablespoon of raw rice. Shake the flask for a few minutes and then rinse.

If you will not be using your flask for a while, pop a couple of lumps of sugar into it to prevent mouldy smells developing.

THREAD

To prevent your double thread tangling when sewing, knot the ends separately instead of together.

TOILET BOWLS

You can easily remove hard water marks inside the toilet bowl by pouring three teacups of vinegar into the bowl and allowing it to soak for a few hours before brushing and flushing.

VACUUM FLASK

When storing a vacuum flask empty, leave the top off to avoid getting a musty smell.

If the flask does smell musty, fill it with a mixture of warm water and two tablespoons of white vinegar, leaving it to stand for several minutes before shaking and rinsing well. If this fails to eliminate the smell, try a mixture of hot water and one and a half tablespoons of bicarbonate of soda. Leave it for at least four hours and rinse well.

WALLPAPER

When storing your rolls of wallpaper, keep them horizontal, not upright as the ends are more likely to get damaged if they are left standing up.

WASHING

To prevent dark clothes from picking up fluff when washing them with other items, turn them inside out before placing them in the machine.

WASHING-UP LIQUID BOTTLE

A clean washing-up liquid bottle filled with water makes an easy to use watering can for small house plants.

WASTE-DISPOSAL UNIT

To clean your waste disposal unit, sprinkle a dozen or so ice cubes with some scouring powder and pass them through it, finishing with a few orange or lemon peels.

WATCHES

If the glass of your watch gets misted up, turn it over and wear the glass next to your skin for a little while. The warmth from your skin will help to clear the mist.

WATERING PLANTS

If you are going away on holiday and can find no one to water your plants, keep them moist by soaking the soil thoroughly and then placing the plant and pot, still dripping, in a polythene bag. Close the bag tightly and place in a position where the plant will receive indirect sunlight.

WEIGHT

When you are keeping an eye on your weight, weigh yourself at the same time of the day once a week. This method will give you a truer idea of any weight loss or gain by counteracting any daily fluctuations.

WINDOWS

When painting window frames, protect the glass from paint by laying strips of dampened newspaper along the edges and in the corners. These will be easy to remove afterwards.

Thoughts for Everyday

"Joy is for all men. It does not depend on circumstance or condition."

Horace Bushnell

"We never know the love of our parents for us till we have become parents."

Henry Ward Beecher

"Most people are about as happy as they make up their minds to be."

Abraham Lincoln

Name ....
Address ....
....
....
Tel ....

Name ....
Address ....
....
....
Tel ....

Name ....
Address ....
....
....
Tel ....

Name ....
Address ....
....
....
Tel ....

Name ....
Address ....
....
....
Tel ....

I

The following details are provided by St. John Ambulance. For a thorough knowledge of first aid, look out for courses held by St. John Ambulance, the British Red Cross and St. Andrew's Ambulance Association.

THE ABC OF RESUSCITATION

A *Open the Airway*

Lift the casualty's jaw and tilt his head to open the airway. Carefully remove any obvious debris from inside his mouth.

B *Check Breathing*

Look to see if his chest is rising and falling. Listen and feel for breath against your cheek.

C *Circulation – Check the Pulse*

Find the pulse in his neck by placing your fingers to the side of his voicebox and pressing gently down.

If pulse and breathing are both present . . .

Turn the casualty into the recovery position.

If there is a pulse but no breathing . . .

Start artificial ventilation. If you must leave him to send for an ambulance, give 10 breaths before going and return quickly to continue.

If there is no pulse and no breathing . . .

Phone for an ambulance, then start chest compressions combined with ventilations.

EMERGENCY AID *

Artificial Ventilation

Pinch casualty's nose firmly.

Take a deep breath and seal your lips around casualty's lips then blow into his mouth watching his chest rise. Let his chest fall completely. Continue at about 10 breaths a minute, checking the pulse after every 10 breaths.

When breathing starts, turn him into the recovery position.

Chest Compression

Give 2 breaths of artificial ventilation. Place the heel of your hand 2 fingers breadth above the

* Never practise on healthy people.

junction of rib margin and breastbone. Place your other hand on top and interlock fingers. Keeping your arms straight press down 4-5 cm (1½-2"), 15 times at a rate of 80 per minute. Repeat cycle (2 breaths to 15 compressions). If condition improves, check the pulse.

RECOVERY POSITION

Turn the casualty onto his side. Keep his head tilted with his jaw forward to maintain the open airway. Check that he cannot roll forwards or backwards. Check his breathing and pulse frequently. If they stop follow the ABC of resuscitation.

CHOKING

A foreign object sticking at the back of the throat may block the throat or induce muscular spasm.

Look out for:

Difficulty in breathing and speaking; blueness of the skin; signs from the casualty – pointing to the throat, or grasping the neck

Your aim is:

To remove the obstruction and restore normal breathing

For an Adult

1. Bend the casualty well forwards and give five sharp slaps between the shoulder blades.
2. If this fails, try abdominal thrusts. The obstruction may be expelled by the sudden pull against the diaphragm.
3. Continue with back slaps and abdominal thrusts alternately.
4. If the casualty becomes unconscious, lay him face down upon the floor. Kneel astride him and perform abdominal thrusts.

If breathing returns, place in the recovery position and call for an ambulance. If it does not, call for an ambulance and begin resuscitation.

For a Casualty who Becomes Unconscious

1. Loss of consciousness may relieve muscle spasm, so check first to see if the casualty can

Thoughts
for
Everyday

"Any cook should be able to run the country."

Lenin

"What matters is not the size of the dog in the fight, but the size of the fight in the dog."

Coach Bear Bryant

"I will speak ill of no man, and speak all the good I know of everybody."

Benjamin Franklin

Name ....

Address ....

....

....

Tel ....

Name ....

Address ....

....

....

Tel ....

Name ....

Address ....

....

....

Tel ....

Name ....

Address ....

....

....

Tel ....

Name ....

Address ....

....

....

Tel ....

J

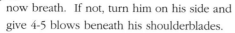

now breath. If not, turn him on his side and give 4-5 blows beneath his shoulderblades.

2. If back blows fail, kneel astride the casualty and perform abdominal thrusts.

If he starts to breathe normally, place in the recovery position and call an ambulance. Check and record breathing and pulse rate every 10 minutes.

If he does not start to breathe again, call for an ambulance and begin resuscitation.

FAINTING

A faint may be a reaction to pain or fright, of the result of emotional upset, exhaustion, or lack of food. It is most common after long periods of physical inactivity, especially in warm atmospheres. Blood pools in the lower part of the body, reducing the amount available to the brain. Recovery from fainting is usually rapid and complete.

Look out for:

A brief loss of consciousness, a slow pulse and pallor

Your aim is:

To improve blood flow to the brain; to reassure the casualty as he recovers, and to make him comfortable

1. Lay the casualty down, and raise and support his legs.
2. Make sure he has plenty of fresh air: open a window if necessary.
3. As he recovers, reassure him and help him sit up gradually.
4. Look for and treat any injury sustained through falling.

If he does not regain consciousness quickly, check breathing and pulse, and be prepared to resuscitate if necessary. Place in the recovery position and call for an ambulance.

If he starts to feel faint again, place his head between his knees and tell him to take deep breaths.

FOREIGN BODIES IN THE SKIN

Your aim is:

To remove the splinter if it protrudes from the skin and to minimise the risk of infection

1. Clean the area around the splinter with soap and warm water. Sterilize a pair of tweezers by passing them through a flame.
2. Grasp the splinter as close to the skin as possible, and draw it out along the tract of its entry.
3. Squeeze the wound to encourage a little bleeding. Clean the area and apply an adhesive dressing.

If the splinter does not come out easily or breaks up, treat as an embedded foreign body. *Never probe the area* (for example, with a needle).

4. Check that the casualty's tetanus immunisation is up to date. If in doubt, advise the casualty to see his doctor.

FOREIGN BODIES IN THE EYE

Look out for:

Blurred vision, pain, or discomfort; redness and watering of the eye; eyelids screwed up in spasm

Your aim is:

To prevent injury to the eye

Do not touch anything sticking to, or embedded in the eyeball, or on the coloured part of the eye. Cover the affected eye with an eye pad, bandage both eyes, then take or send the casualty to hospital.

If the object is on the white of the eye, and not stuck:

1. Advise the casualty not to rub his eye. Sit him down facing the light.
2. Gently separate the eyelids with your finger and thumb. Examine every part of his eye.
3. If you can see the foreign body, wash it out using a glass or an eye irrigator, and clean water (sterile, if possible).
4. If this is unsuccessful then, providing the foreign body is not stuck in place, lift it off with a moist swab, or the damp corner of a tissue or clean handkerchief.

Thoughts
for
Everyday

"If you judge people, you have no time to love them."

Mother Teresa

"You can fool some of the people all of the time, and all of the people some of the time, but you cannot fool all of the people all of the time."

Ascribed to Abraham Lincoln

"All the beautiful sentiments in the world weigh less than a single lovely action."

James Russell Lowell

Name ....

Address ....

....

....

Tel ....

Name ....

Address ....

....

....

Tel ....

Name ....

Address ....

....

....

Tel ....

Name ....

Address ....

....

....

Tel ....

Name ....

Address ....

....

....

Tel ....

J

If the object is under the eyelid, grasping the lashes, pull the upper lid over the lower lid. Blinking the eye under water may also make the object float clear.

FOREIGN BODIES IN THE NOSE

Look out for:

Difficulty in breathing, or noisy breathing, through the nose; swelling of the nose; smelly or blood-stained discharge indicating an object present for some time

Your aim is:

To obtain medical attention

Do not attempt to remove the foreign body – you may cause injury

1. Keep the casualty quiet. Advise him to breathe through the mouth.
2. Take or send the casualty to hospital.

FOREIGN BODIES IN THE EAR

Your aim is:

To prevent injury to the ear and to obtain medical aid if necessary

For a lodged foreign body

Do not attempt to remove the object. You may cause serious injury or push the object in further. Take or send the casualty to hospital. Reassure him during transport or until help arrives.

For an insect in the ear

1. Sit the casualty down.
2. Gently flood the ear with tepid water so that the insect floats out.
3. If this is unsuccessful, take or send the casualty to hospital.

HOUSEHOLD POISONS

Almost every household contains poisonous substances, such as bleach, paint stripper, glue, paraffin, and weedkiller, which can be spilled, causing chemical burns, or swallowed. Children in particular are at risk from accidental household poisoning.

Preventing Poisoning in the Home

+ Keep dangerous chemicals out of children's reach (not under the sink)
+ Keep medicines in a locked cupboard
+ Leave poisonous household substances in their original containers
+ Buy medicines and household substances in tamper-proof containers

Your aim is:

To maintain airway, breathing, and circulation; to obtain medical aid; and to identify the poison

For Chemicals on the Skin

1. Wash away any residual chemical on the skin with plenty of water.

   Do not contaminate yourself with the dangerous chemical or the rinsing water.
2. Use your judgement to call a doctor or call for an ambulance. Give information about the spilled chemical.

For Swallowed Poisons

1. Check and, if necessary, clear the airway.

   If the casualty is unconscious, check breathing and pulse, and be prepared to resuscitate. If artificial ventilation is necessary, a plastic face shield will protect you if there is burning around the mouth.

Place the casualty in the recovery position: he may well vomit.

Do not try to induce vomiting.

2. Use your judgement to call a doctor or call for an ambulance. Give information about the swallowed poison.

If a conscious casualty's lips are burned by corrosive substances, give him frequent sips of cold water or milk.

INSECT STINGS

+ If the sting is visible, gently remove with tweezers.
+ Apply a cold pad, surgical spirit or a solution of bicarbonate of soda.

GAS

IF YOU SMELL GAS

- Put out cigarettes. Do not use matches or naked flames.
- Do not operate electrical switches—either on or off.
- Open doors and windows to let the gas escape.
- Check to see if a tap has been left on accidentally or if a pilot light has gone out.
- If not, there is probably a gas leak. So turn off the whole supply at the meter and call gas service.

ELECTRICITY

POWER CUTS

Make things easier for yourself by planning for power cuts. Keep a good supply of candles, matches, torches and lamps (and fuel) in a place where you can find them easily in the dark. You might consider buying a calor gas or paraffin heater and/or a calor gas camping stove for such instances.

- Switch off lights and electrical appliances such as blankets, fires and cookers as they could cause an accident when the power is switched back on.
- Leave the fridge and freezer switched on, but check that the fridge drip tray is in position and keep the door closed. The freezer contents should remain unharmed for at least 8 hours but it might be an idea to insure your freezer contents anyway.
- Never let children carry candles unless accompanied by an adult. Give them a torch instead.
- When the power is restored remember to extinguish all candles.
- Reset all electric clocks including those which control central heating.

FIRE

WHAT TO DO IF FIRE BREAKS OUT

Remember that smoke can kill as well as flames. If there is smoke, or whenever the fire is too big to tackle quickly and safely:

- Get everyone out of the house at once
- Shut all doors behind you
- Call the Fire Service

If you are trapped in a room

- Keep the door shut.
- Put a blanket or carpet at the bottom of the door.
- Go to the window and call for help.

If you have to escape

- Throw a mattress out of the window and lower yourself out of the window – feet first. Hold on to the sill with your hands and drop onto the mattress.

CHIP PAN FIRES

- Switch off the heat.
- Smother the pan with a large lid or damp cloth.
- Don't move the pan or throw water on it.

ELECTRICAL FIRES

- Switch off at the socket and unplug.
- Never use water while the power is on.
- Use a dry powder extinguisher to put out the fire.

FLOODING

NATURAL DISASTER

Emergency services automatically move into operation when an area is flooded or likely to flood through adverse weather or other natural conditions. Switch off your electricity supply at the mains if it is accessible (make sure your hands are dry), if possible move on to an upper floor and wait for help to arrive.

Untitled

Come, the wind may never again
Blow as now it blows for us;
And the stars may never again
   shine as now they shine;
Long before October returns,
Seas of blood will have parted us;
And you must crush the love in
   your heart, and I the love in
   mine!

Emily Bronte

The Revelation

An idle poet, here and there,
Looks round him; but,
  for all the rest,
The world, unfathomably fair,
Is duller than a witling's jest.
Love wakes men, once a lifetime
  each;
They lift their heavy lids, and look;
They read with joy, then shut
  the book.
And some give thanks,
  and some blaspheme,
And most forget; but, either way,
That and the Child's unheeded
  dream
Is all the light of all their day.

Coventry Patmore

Name ....
Address ....
....
....
Tel ....

Name ....
Address ....
....
....
Tel ....

Name ....
Address ....
....
....
Tel ....

Name ....
Address ....
....
....
Tel ....

Name ....
Address ....
....
....
Tel ....

K

	MEASLES	WHOOPING COUGH	MUMPS	CHICKENPOX	GERMAN MEASLES (Rubella)	GASTRO-ENTERITIS
INCUBATION PERIOD	8 to 10 days before the running nose and head cold, 14 days before the appearance of the rash.	8 to 14 days.	14 to 28 days.	10 to 25 days.	14 to 21 days.	1 to 7 days; varies with different germs.
EARLY SYMPTOMS	Starts with a running nose, bleary eyes and a hard cough. The doctor will look inside the mouth for minute white spots which appear 2 or 3 days before the rash.	Starts with "chestiness" and a simple cough. This later becomes spasmodic with "paroxysms" ending with a whoop and/or vomiting.	Generally off colour for a few days before they complain of pain or soreness on chewing.	First sign of the illness is usually the detection of spots on the trunk when the child is being bathed or undressed.	Some throat discomfort and slight fever at onset but the appearance of the rash is often the first sign of the disease. Painful swollen glands at the back of the head.	Nausea and vomiting often followed by diarrhoea. There may be fever.
DISTINCTIVE FEATURES	The rash appears 3 or 4 days after the first symptoms and begins behind the ears, spreads downwards to the body and lower limbs. It consists of dark, purplish, spots which run together to make blotchy areas. The eyes are always reddened.	When fully developed diagnosis is obvious. Hurried breathing denotes onset of pneumonia. This may occur early in young children who have not been immunised and may leave permanent lung damage. Children with severe or frequent vomiting need more food after a paroxysm.	The salivary gland below the ear and behind the angle of the jaw is swollen and painful on pressure. The gland on the opposite side may be involved up to 7 days later. Boys after puberty may develop painful swelling of the testicles. Mild, transient meningitis is quite common, but it does not usually need special treatment.	The spots become "blistery" then yellow and form scabs. There may be several "crops" of spots.	The rash consists of pink flat spots which merge together to give a "peachbloom" appearance. There is no red throat or pallor round the mouth.	Vomiting rarely lasts more than a day or two, but diarrhoea may persist. Crampy stomach pains are common, but very severe stomach ache, or blood in more than 2 or 3 motions need checking on by the doctor.
DURATION	Allow for a few days in bed and 2 weeks before they can return to school.	A severe attack will require at least 6 weeks before return to school but mild cases sometimes occur in children who have been immunised.	Only severe cases need to be confined to bed. Return to school after the swelling has subsided.	A child is no longer infectious as soon as ALL the spots have dried to scabs.	Uneventful recovery within 6 days. All German Measles patients should be isolated from pregnant women.	Usually 1 to 4 days. Severe cases may last many days. Solid foods need not be given until diarrhoea improves.
NURSING POINTS	The mouth needs special care with mouthwashes or swabbing after food. Shortness of breath as rash fades, persistent severe earache and very inflamed eyes usually require medical advice.	The small infant requires special care during paroxysms and should be lifted out of the cot and held head downwards until the spasm ceases. Older children should be calmed and reassured but can cope with their own spasms.	Careful washing of the mouth after a meal is important to remove all crumbs.	It is almost impossible to prevent the child from scratching the irritable spots so finger-nails should be kept short.	The course of the disease is usually uneventful. Some patients develop pain and swelling in the small joints of the hands. This will subside.	Babies do best on frequent small breast feeds and plenty of boiled water. Otherwise make up electrolyte powder or tablets (from the chemist) in boiled water. Watered-down fizzy drinks may also be accepted by older children.

Thoughts for Everyday

"Happiness is not the absence of problems; but the ability to deal with them."

Author Unidentified

"A smooth sea never made a skillful mariner."

English Proverb

"Early rising not only gives us more life in the same number of years, but adds, likewise, to their number."

Charles Cotton

Name ....

Address ....

....

....

Tel ....

Name ....

Address ....

....

....

Tel ....

Name ....

Address ....

....

....

Tel ....

Name ....

Address ....

....

....

Tel ....

Name ....

Address ....

....

....

Tel ....

K

Kitchen Information

DRY WEIGHT

Approximate gram conversion to nearest round figure	Recommended gram conversion to nearest 25g	Imperial ounce (oz)	
28	25	1	
57	50	2	
85	75	3	
113	100-125	4	(¼ lb)
142	150	5	
170	175	6	
198	200	7	
227	225	8	(½ lb)
255	250	9	
284	275	10	
311	300	11	
340	350	12	(¾ lb)
368	375	13	
396	400	14	
425	425	15	
453	450	16	(1lb)

LIQUID MEASURES

Approx. ml conversion*	Recommended ml equivalent	Imperial pint	Imperial fluid ounce (oz)
568	575-600	1	20
284	300	½	10
142	150	¼	5

** to nearest round figure*

QUICK HANDY MEASURES

Approximately equivalent for 25g (1oz) shown in level 15ml (1tbsp) spoonfuls.

Almonds, ground	3 ½
Breadcrumbs, dried	3
Breadcrumbs, fresh	7
Butter/Lard	2
Cheddar, grated	3
Chocolate, grated	4
Coffee, instant	6 ½
Cornflour	2 ¾
Curry Powder	4
Custard Powder	2 ¾
Flour, unsifted	3
Sugar, caster/granulated	2
Sugar, demerara	2
Sugar, icing	3
Syrup or honey	1

METRIC PACKS

Remember that:

25g is slightly less than 1 oz

125g is slightly more than ¼ lb

250g is slightly more than ½ lb

500g is slightly more than 1 lb

1kg is slightly more than 2 ¼ lb

COOKING (DIAL MARKINGS)

Gasmark	¼	1	2	3	4
Fahrenheit	250	275	300	325	350
Celsius	120	140	150	160	180

Gasmark	5	6	7	8	9
Fahrenheit	375	400	425	450	475
Celsius	190	200	220	230	240

LIQUID TEMPERATURES

(water, milk, etc)

Boiling Point	100°C	212°F
Simmering	96°C	205°F
Tepid	37°C	96°F
Freezing Point	0°C	32°F

OVEN TEMPERATURES

Gasmark	Description
1/4	Very Slow
1/2	Very Slow
1	Slow
2	Slow
3	Moderate
4	Moderate
5	Moderately Hot
6	Moderately Hot
7	Hot
8	Hot
9	Very Hot

TEMPERATURE CONVERSION CHART

°F	°C
212B	100B
122	50
113	45
104	40
95	35
86	30
77	25
68	20
59	15
50	10
41	5
32	0
23	-5
14	-10
5	-15
-4	-20

Conversions given are approximate. Never mix metric and imperial measures in one recipe – stick to one system or the other.

Thoughts for Everyday

"Whatever is worth doing at all is worth doing well."

Lord Chesterfield

"Education is what survives when what has been learnt has been forgotten."

B F Skinner

"A group of two hundred executives were asked what makes a person successful. Eighty per cent listed enthusiasm as the most important quality."

Author Unidentified

Name ....

Address ....

....

....

Tel ....

Name ....

Address ....

....

....

Tel ....

Name ....

Address ....

....

....

Tel ....

Name ....

Address ....

....

....

Tel ....

Name ....

Address ....

....

....

Tel ....

L

WHAT IS A HEALTHY DIET?

Eating for health does not need to be extreme: it is a matter of common sense and moderation. Here are some facts and advice on nutrition which you can use to gauge your own diet and see if there is any way you can make it healthier.

FOOD FOR LIVING

People are becoming aware that one of the keys to healthy living is a healthy balanced diet. The chart below illustrates the four main food groups. By choosing food from each of the groups daily, you will be most likely to get sufficient energy, protein, fibre, and important vitamins and minerals.

MILK & DAIRY FOODS	HIGH PROTEIN FOODS
Milk, Yogurt *Cheese* *Fromage Frais*	*Red Meat, Chicken,* *Fish, Eggs, Pulses* *Nuts & Seeds, Tofu*
FRUIT & VEGETABLES	POTATOES & CEREALS
Green Vegetables *Root Vegetables* *Fruit, Fruit Juices*	*Bread, Pasta* *Rice, Potatoes* *Breakfast Cereal*

Try to have twice as much from the Fruit and Vegetables category and the Potatoes and Cereals categories as from the other two groups. Growing children and pregnant women or those breastfeeding will also need larger portions from the Milk and Dairy group to supply extra calcium requirements. It is generally recognised nowadays that poultry and fish are healthy substitutes for a heavy red meat diet.

VEGETARIANISM

Increasingly, many people are adopting a vegetarian diet. If you do make this choice, then it is important to be aware of your nutrient requirements, and which foods to eat to still maintain a healthy balanced diet. If you wish very young children to follow an extreme vegetarian diet, such as veganism, it would be wise to consult a doctor first, to ensure that they are eating the right foods to meet their needs.

LOWER FAT

Cut down on fried foods.

Choose larger portions of vegetables rather than extra helpings of fatty foods.

Cut the fat off meat and the skin off chicken.

Spread butter or margarine very thinly (or use a low-fat spread).

Choose yogurt or fruit instead of rich puddings.

Try yogurt as a dressing or half and half with cream on desserts.

Cut down on biscuits, chocolates and savoury snacks.

Try semi-skimmed milk in sauces, or as a drink.

LOWER SUGAR

Gradually reduce the amount added to drinks.

Choose 'Diet' versions of fizzy drinks.

Try unsweetened varieties of breakfast cereals.

HIGHER FIBRE

Eat more bread, pasta and potatoes.

Choose wholemeal varieties of bread and pasta.

Start the day with a high fibre breakfast cereal, porridge or muesli.

Use more beans, e.g add kidney beans to a stew, try lentils in a rissole or meat loaf.

Peas, sweetcorn, apricots, figs and bananas are good sources of fibre.

LOWER SALT

Cook vegetables without salt.

Don't add salt automatically: taste first.

Use fresh herbs to add flavour to your cooking.

Keep tabs on the amount of salty and pickled foods you eat.

Thoughts *for* *Everyday*

"When all men praised the peacock for his tail, the birds cried out 'Look at his legs! and what a voice!' "

Japanese Proverb

"It's a funny thing about life; if you refuse to accept anything but the best, you very often get it."

Somerset Maugham

"He that is good for making excuses is seldom good for anything else."

Benjamin Franklin

Name ....
Address ....
....
....
Tel ....

Name ....
Address ....
....
....
Tel ....

Name ....
Address ....
....
....
Tel ....

Name ....
Address ....
....
....
Tel ....

Name ....
Address ....
....
....
Tel ....

L

A Healthy Diet

There are about 30 vitamins and minerals which are essential for the body. Many are required in very small quantities or are so widely distributed in foods that deficiencies are rarely seen in Britain. For most healthy people, a well balanced and varied diet provides adequate vitamins and minerals without the need for pills or tonics.

To help in planning a balanced diet, the following table gives a guide to where the major vitamins and minerals can be found:—

NUTRIENT	ADULT RECOMMENDED DAILY AMOUNT	FUNCTION	FACTS
Vitamin A	750µg	Vision in dim light Healthy skin	1/4oz of liver or small carrot provide over 100% of the RDA
Vitamin B Complex Thiamin (B1) Riboflavin (B2) Nicotinic acid (B3)	(B1) 1.0mg (B2) 1.3-1.7mg (B3) 15-18mg No RDA set	Conversion of food to energy in cells	Many breakfast cereals and some breads are fortified with B vitamins
Vitamin B12	No RDA set	Formation of bone marrow and blood cells	Milk is a valuable source for vegetarians
Vitamin C	30mg	Healthy tissues Assists iron absorption	Half a glass of orange juice provides over 30mg
Vitamin D	10µg (for under 5's and pregnant women and breastfeeding women only)	Bone formation Deficiency can cause rickets or osteomalacia	Sunlight is a major source
Calcium	500mg 1200mg in late pregnancy and lactation	Bone formation and maintenance throughout all your life	A glass of milk, a pot of yogurt and an ounce of cheese each provide about 250mg
Iron		Oxygen transport in blood	Better absorbed when vitamin C also present

HOW TO MINIMISE NUTRIENT LOSSES IN COOKING

DO
✓ Use vegetables, fruit and fruit juices when fresh. (Frozen vegetables can be as nutritious as fresh).
✓ Use minimum amounts of water (eg 2cm in pan or steam/microwave).
✓ Consume promptly.

DON'T
✗ Chop vegetables finely hours before cooking
✗ Overcook vegetables.
✗ Add baking soda or bicarbonate (destroys B vitamins).

MILK, CHEESE & YOGHURT

These are our major source of calcium – important throughout life for growth and strength of bones.

MEAT

This is an excellent source of protein, iron (particularly red meat), zinc and a range of B vitamins. The iron is easily absorbed and does not benefit from the presence of vitamin C for absorption.

POULTRY

Chicken and other poultry are a good source of protein and contain iron and a range of B vitamins. The white meat of roast chicken and turkey is particularly low in fat if eaten without the skin. The dark meat of the legs and around the back-bone is higher in fat.

LIVER, KIDNEY & HEART

Particularly rich in iron and vitamin A, as well as providing protein and a range of B vitamins.

FISH

White fish provides protein and is relatively fat free and low in calories – unless you fry it!
Oily fish – mackerel, herrings, kippers, sardines – are a good source of protein and vitamin D. Tinned fish is a good source of calcium – as long as you eat the bones!

EGGS

Eggs provide protein, iron and most of the B vitamins. Though containing cholesterol, they are low in fat and are a useful source of vitamins A and D.
The iron in eggs is better absorbed if a vitamin C rich food – citrus fruit or juice or potatoes – is eaten at the same meal. Caffeine – in coffee, tea and cola drinks – tends to reduce its absorption.

PULSES

Lentils and other dried beans such as red kidney, black-eye and haricot are good sources of protein, particularly in a vegetarian/vegan diet. They are high in fibre, low in fat and provide iron, B vitamins and some calcium. Baked beans, low in sugar, are now available.

NUTS

Nuts are protein rich but are also relatively high in fat, calories and, if salted, in salt. The fat is unsaturated and a good source of vitamin E.

FRUITS & VEGETABLES

The high water content of most of these foods together with their plant origin means they are relatively low in calories and, particularly if unpeeled, a useful source of fibre. Many are good sources of vitamin C although, if canned, some of this will be transferred to the canning juices.

POTATOES & ROOT VEGETABLES

Potatoes are a good source of fibre – particularly if the skins are eaten – and of vitamin C. Peeling and cutting potatoes, then cooking in lots of water causes high losses of vitamin C, so baking is the ideal cooking method. Carrots are an excellent source of vitamin A. Swede, if cooked as for leafy vegetables, is a good source of vitamin C.

from L' Allegro

Night hath better sweets to prove
Venus now wakens and wakens
    love,
Come, let us our rites begin;
'Tis only daylight that makes sin.

John Milton

Oh, No – Not Ev'n When We First Lov'd

Oh, no–not ev'n when first we lov'd
Wert thou as dear as now thou art;
Thy beauty then my senses mov'd
But now thy virtues bind my heart.
What was but Passion's sigh before
Has since been turn'd to Reason's
    vow;
And, though I then might love
    thee more,
Trust me, I love thee better now.

Although my heart in earlier youth
Might kindle with more wild desire,
Believe me, it has gain'd in truth
Much more than it has lost in fire.
The flame now warms my inmost
    core
That then but sparkled o'er my brow
And though I seem'd to love thee
    more
Yet, oh, I love thee better now.

Thomas Moore

Name ....
Address ....
....
....
Tel ....

Name ....
Address ....
....
....
Tel ....

Name ....
Address ....
....
....
Tel ....

Name ....
Address ....
....
....
Tel ....

Name ....
Address ....
....
....
Tel ....

M

CITRUS FRUIT

Oranges, satsumas, lemons and grapefruit are excellent sources of vitamin C. Check the labels on cans and cartons of these juices to see whether they contain vitamin C – sometimes it can be lost during processing. Unless fortified, citrus fruit drinks rarely contain vitamin C.

APPLES, PEARS, PLUMS

These types of fruit contain principally water, natural sugars and, particularly if unpeeled, dietary fibre.

TROPICAL FRUITS

Pineapples, melons and kiwi fruit are a good source of vitamin C.

Bananas, although not rich in vitamin C, are a useful source because the average banana weighs 5-8oz (150-225g). Mango, paw paws, peaches and orange coloured melons contain vitamin A.

SOFT FRUITS

Strawberries and raspberries are useful sources of vitamin C. Freezing preserves vitamin C and so picking and freezing is a useful way to enjoy the benefits of strawberries all year round.

CREAM

Fresh cream varies in fat content between 12% and 55%. Although it provides vitamin A, the quantities consumed and fre-quency with which most people eat it, in reality, mean cream is an insignificant source of fat or vitamin A in most people's diet.

BUTTER

Butter is approximately 81% fat and contains vitamins A and D.

MARGARINE

Like butter, hard and soft margarine contains 81% fat. It is fortified with vitamins A and D. The type of fat it contains varies considerably.

OILS & LARD

Though different types of fat, both vegetable oils and lard are virtually 100% fat. A tablespoon of oil therefore contains as much fat as 1 oz (25g) butter or margarine.

Some vegetable oils contain vitamin E but rarely contain vitamins A or D.

SPREADS & BUTTER SUBSTITUTES

Low fat spreads contain about half the fat of butter or margarine. As this is an ever developing market, read carefully the label of the brand of your choice.

Thoughts for Everyday

"I like the dreams of the future better than the history of the past."

Thomas Jefferson

"The proper office of a friend is to side with you when you are in the wrong. Nearly anybody will side with you when you are in the right."

Mark Twain

"Gratefulness is the poor man's payment."

English Proverb

Name ....
Address ....
....
....
Tel ....

Name ....
Address ....
....
....
Tel ....

Name ....
Address ....
....
....
Tel ....

Name ....
Address ....
....
....
Tel ....

Name ....
Address ....
....
....
Tel ....

M

HERBS

Herbs play an essential role in any kitchen, adding flavour and distinction to many dishes. All are available fresh or dried but remember that fresh herbs have a milder flavour and use roughly 15ml (1 tablespoon) of fresh herbs to 5ml (1 teaspoon) of dried.

Basil (Ocimum basilicum)

Two types of basil are grown; sweet and bush. The one most commonly found is sweet basil, which has largish, shiny, green leaves and a strong but sweet flavour. It is one of the best herbs to add to tomatoes, eggs, mushrooms and pasta dishes, forms part of a classic bouquet garni, and is an essential part of pesto sauce. Basil does not dry very successfully.

Bay Leaves (Laurus nobilis)

Sweet bay or bay laurel is a Mediterranean tree. The leaves are shiny, smooth and dark with a strong aromatic scent. It is often added to stocks when poaching fish, or to marinades, casseroles, soups and stews. It can also be used to flavour milk puddings.

Chervil (Anthriscus cerefolium)

Chervil is a member of the parsley family and is very popular with French chefs. It has a delicate fern-like leaf, offering a delicate taste with a hint of anise. It is especially good in soups, egg and cheese dishes, or added for flavour to green salad. It can also be used as a garnishing leaf.

Chives (Allium schoenoprasum)

A member of the onion family, chives have a mild onion flavour and long, spiky, green leaves. Raw chives are frequently used in salads, but can be added to omelettes, cheese dishes, and, mixed with soured cream, used as a topping for baked potatoes.

Coriander (Coriandrum sativum)

Coriander has flat feathery leaves and is often confused with flat parsley. It has a distinctive spicy flavour and is popular in Southern European, Indian and South East Asian cooking. The leaves are chopped and added to curries, stews, soups and marinades. It is also known as Chinese or Japanese parsley, and is used in the same way as parsley.

Dill (Anethum graveolens)

A delicate, feathery herb with an aromatic, sharp but sweet flavour. One of the most popular herbs in Scandinavia, it is especially good with fish if added to the marinade, cooking liquid or accompanying sauces. It can also be added to vegetables, cream or cottage cheese.

Lemon Balm (Melissa officinalis)

The crushed leaves of this plant, as the name would suggest, give off a wonderful lemony scent, making them ideal for use in salads.

Marjoram (Origanum majorana)

Sweet marjoram, a plant native to the Mediterranean, has small, furry leaves and a flavour similar to oregano but sweeter and milder. It can be added to most savoury dishes and is good with marrow, potatoes and rice.

It is very fragrant and can be dried successfully.

Mint (Menta spp.)

There are many species of this popular herb, from spearmint to the fresh-tasting peppermint used for tisanes. It is probably the best known herb in Britain and most commonly used with lamb and new potatoes. It can also be added to other young vegetables or chopped with minced beef, or mixed with yogurt for a dip. It also combines well with fruit.

Thoughts for Everyday

"Dishonesty is like a boomerang. About the time you think all is well, it hits you in the back of the head."

Author Unidentified

"Happiness makes up in height for what it lacks in length."

Robert Frost

"Give a man a fish and you feed him for one day. Teach a man to fish and you feed him for a lifetime."

Chinese Proverb

Name ....

Address ....

....

....

Tel ....

Name ....

Address ....

....

....

Tel ....

Name ....

Address ....

....

....

Tel ....

Name ....

Address ....

....

....

Tel ....

Name ....

Address ....

....

....

Tel ....

Oregano (Origanum vulgare)

Oregano is wild marjoram, and, as it has the best flavour when grown in strong sun, is popular in Mediterranean cuisines – especially those of Italy and Greece. The flavour is similar to marjoram but stronger and the leaves are larger and darker. It enhances many meat dishes and it is often added to salads, pizza and tomato based dishes. Oregano can be dried successfully, keeping all its aroma.

Parsley (Petroselinum crispum)

There are two types of parsley: curled and flat. Flat (or French) parsley is generally grown in Europe and is considered to have a finer taste than curled parsley, but both are strong in Vitamin C and iron. Parsley is an essential part of a bouquet garni. It enlivens most savoury dishes and is often simply used as a garnish, either chopped or as sprigs. The chopped leaves can be added to salads, soups, sauces and cooked vegetables. It is said that if chewed after eating garlic it will remove the smell.

Rosemary (Rosmarinus officinalis)

A pungent, fragrant shrub with small, narrow leaves, set densely on the branches. It is often used with lamb but can be used with other meats and in vegetable dishes such as ratatouille or added to marinades.

Sage (Salvia officinalis)

Sage comes in many varieties and is a strongly flavoured herb with narrow, pale grey-green leaves with a rough texture. It has traditionally been used with pork, liver, and in stuffing, but can be used with any richly flavoured meat, and in cheese and tomato dishes. It dries well but can become musty if kept too long.

Savory (Satureja)

There are two varieties of savory: Winter savory (Satureja montana), and Summer savory (Satureja hortensis). The German name for winter savory means "bean-herb", indicating its traditional use, while summer savory is similar and even more aromatic.

Tarragon (Artemisia dracunculus)

There are two varieties of this herb: French and Russian. The French variety is harder to grow but is far more aromatic than the Russian. It has a distinctive flavour and shiny narrow leaves. It is widely used in vinegars, soups, stuffings, sauces, and salad dressings, and is also good with roast meat, poultry dishes and fish.

Thyme (Thymus vulgaris)

This popular herb contains an essential oil, thymol, which helps to digest fatty foods. Its small, dark-green bushy leaves have a very strong flavour.

It is another herb which should be used in a bouquet garni, and it can be used to flavour meat, fish, soups, stews and vegetables.

Thoughts for Everyday

"Nothing great was ever achieved without enthusiasm. The way of life is wonderful; it is by abandonment."

Ralph Waldo Emerson

"The most wasted day is that in which we have not laughed."

Chamfort

"When you tell the truth, you never have to worry about your lousy memory."

Author Unidentified

Name ....

Address ....

....

....

Tel ....

Name ....

Address ....

....

....

Tel ....

Name ....

Address ....

....

....

Tel ....

Name ....

Address ....

....

....

Tel ....

Name ....

Address ....

....

....

Tel ....

N

SPICES

Spices are the dried parts of aromatic plants and may be the fruit, root, flower, bud, bark or seed. For the best flavour, grind your own spices just before use.

Aniseed (Pimpinella asinum)

Aniseed has a strong liquorice flavour and is popular in Mexico and all over the Mediterranean.

Capers (Capparis spinosa)

The buds of a small Mediterranean bush, these are usually sold pickled in vinegar and should not be allowed to dry out. While they are used mostly in sauces and salads, they are also popular as a pizza topping, adding an authentic Mediterranean flavour.

Caraway (Carum carvi)

Caraway is in appearance similar to cumin seed and because of this is often confused with it. The taste, however, is very different.

Cardamom (Elettaria cardamomum)

Cardamom is a relative of the ginger family, available both whole green, black or white or ground. The most common is the grey-green pod which contains minute, dark brown seeds with an unmistakable bitter-sweet flavour with a hint of lemon and eucalyptus. It is used extensively in sweet and savoury Indian cookery as well as in Europe and the Middle East as an ingredient in cakes, biscuits and pickles and to flavour drinks.

Chili (Capsicum frutescens)

Ripe chili peppers dry and keep well and are most commonly used in chili powder, a very hot spice, whose blend may vary due to the numerous varieties of chilies to be found. Cayenne is a very hot, pungent red chili sold ready ground. Milder chili powders can be found or you can use chili seasoning which is a blend of ground dried chilis with other spices. It is used (sparingly) in meat, fish, poultry and egg dishes as well as soups, sauces and pickles.

Cinnamon (Cinnamomum zeylanicum)

The distinctive sticks of dried bark are harvested from the young shoots of a large, tropical evergreen. While it is best purchased as sticks and used whole or ground, is also available as a powder and has a sweet pungent flavour. Cinnamon is usually added to savoury dishes in the East and to sweet dishes in the West, and is used in apple desserts, cakes and mulled drinks.

Cloves (Eugenia caryophyllata)

Cloves are the unopened flower buds of the tropical evergreen clove tree. They become rich brown in colour when dried and resemble small nails in shape. Cloves have a penetrating taste and are available whole or ground: if used whole then they are best removed before a dish is eaten. They are used mainly to flavour fruit dishes, mulled wine, mincemeat, bread sauce and curries.

Coriander (Coriandrum sativum)

Coriander is a member of the parsley family. The aromatic brown seeds have a sweet orangey flavour. Sold whole or ground, they are quite mild so can be used more freely than most spices and are used widely in Arab and Eastern cookery; in curries, casseroles, soups, dishes such as couscous and hummus and with vegetables and chutneys.

Cumin (Cuminum cyminum)

Cumin is a member of the parsley family and is available both as seeds or in powdered form. It has a sharp, spicy, slightly bitter taste and should be used in moderation. It is often combined with coriander as a basic curry mixture, but is also used for flavouring Middle Eastern fish recipes, casseroles and couscous. It can be added to pickles, chutneys, soups and rice dishes.

Ginger (Zingiber officinale)

Ginger is a distinctive knobbly root with a hot sweetish taste sold in several forms. Fresh root ginger, essential for many Eastern recipes, releases its true flavour on cooking. It is peeled and then sliced or grated for use in curries, Chinese cooking or marinades for meat, fish and poultry. Dried ginger is the dried ground root and is best used in preserves, cakes, biscuits and puddings. Stem ginger is available preserved in syrup or crystallized and is a sweetmeat either eaten whole, with carel, or used in breads, cakes, confectionery and desserts.

Juniper (Juniperus communis)

Juniper berries have a pungent, slightly resinous flavour. They go well with cabbage and add a light touch to oily or heavy dishes.

Mace (Myristica fragrans)

Mace is the dried outer membrane of nutmeg. It is sold both as blades or ground, although ground mace quickly loses its flavour. It is used in mulled wines and punches, meat pies, loaves, stews, savoury white sauces and in milk puddings.

Nutmeg (Myristica fragrans)

Nutmeg has a brown uneven outer surface with a pale interior, is milder than mace although slightly nuttier and is available whole or ground, but as it loses its flavour quickly, is best grated as required. It can be sprinkled on vegetables and is used in soups, sauces, meat terrines, pates, and puddings.

Paprika (Capsicum annum)

A finely ground red powder made from the fruits of several chili plants, popular in Hungary and Spain. The flesh only is used for mild sweet paprikas whilst the seeds are included in more pungent paprikas. Use to add colour to egg and cheese dishes, in salads, with fish and shellfish, chicken and classically in Hungarian Goulash.

Saffron (Crocus sativus)

Saffron is the dried stigmas of the saffron crocus flower. It is very expensive, as it is individually handpicked and imparts a slightly bitter honey-like flavour and a yellow colour. It is safer to buy the threads as the powder is easy to adulterate. It is added to rice dishes, Spanish Paella, Bouillabaisse and to Cornish Saffron cake.

Turmeric (Circuma longa)

Turmeric is the dried root of a plant from the ginger family, usually sold ground, although sometimes sold fresh. It has a strong woody aroma and a slightly bitter flavour and is used to colour rice, pickles, cakes and in curries and dhals. It is sometimes used as a cheap substitute for saffron to colour dishes, but the flavour is not the same.

Vanilla (Vanilla planifolia)

Vanilla is the fruit of an orchid plant found in Mexico. It has traditionally been used to flavour chocolate, and is good in many sweet dishes, though it is expensive to buy.

Song

How sweet I roam'd from field
   to field,
And tasted all the summer's pride,
Till I the prince of love beheld,
Who in the sunny beams did glide!

He shew'd me lilies for my hair,
And blushing roses for my brow;
He led me through his gardens fair,
Where all his golden pleasures grow.

With sweet May dews my wings
   were wet,
And Phoebus fir'd my vocal rage;
He caught me in his silken net,
And shut me in his golden cage.

He loves to sit and hear me sing,
Then, laughing, sports and plays
   with me;
Then stretches out my golden wing,
And mocks my loss of liberty.

William Blake

Ae Fond Kiss

Had we never loved sae kindly,
Had we never loved sae blindly,
Never met—or never parted,
We had ne'er been broken-hearted.

Robert Burns

Name ....

Address ....

....

....

Tel ....

Name ....

Address ....

....

....

Tel ....

Name ....

Address ....

....

....

Tel ....

Name ....

Address ....

....

....

Tel ....

Name ....

Address ....

....

....

Tel ....

O

Unusual Vegetables

Pumpkin

The pumpkin, with its bright orange flesh and skin, is one of the largest of the squashes, and can be used both as a fruit and vegetable. Pumpkins may weigh up to 68kg (150lb), although they are more usually 3-13kg (7-29lb). They contains 15 calories per 100g (4oz) and are a good source of vitamin A.

To serve, halve and scoop out the seeds. Cut into sections, peel and chop the flesh into even-sized pieces. Cook in boiling, lightly salted water until tender, steam or roast. Use in stews or in sweet dishes such as jams and pie fillings.

Oyster Mushrooms

These are found growing naturally in woodlands during autumn, early winter and spring. They have been used in Chinese, European and Indian cuisine for years and are now being cultivated for sale. To serve, wipe if necessary, but do not wash or peel. They are extremely versatile and can bee cooked in a variety of ways.

Custard Marrow

The custard marrow is a member of the squash family. It is a yellow disc-shaped summer squash with a scalloped edge, resembling a fluted yellow custard pie. It is best eaten young, at about 10cm (4 inches) in diameter and tastes similar to courgettes, and can in fact be served stuffed with a savoury filling, like courgettes. Alternatively, bake au gratin, add to soups or stews, or serve raw in salads.

Jerusalem Artichokes

These are tubers which were originally grown in North America, but were introduced into France in the 17th century and then into the UK. They are not related to globe artichokes.

The tubers are misshapen, knobbly and irregular in shape with light beigy brown skins. They contain 41 calories per 100g (4oz) boiled. To cook, scrub, boil or steam, and peel if necessary. Serve with a butter or wine sauce, or cook in gratins, soups or roast.

Shittake Mushrooms

The name Shittake is Japanese, meaning forest mushrooms. They are highly regarded throughout the Far East and are now cultivated in North America and the UK and vary in colour from creamy brown to dark chestnut. They have a softer flesh than button mushrooms and a much meatier type of flavour.

To serve, wipe if necessary, but do not wash or peel. Cut away most of the stalk and leave whole or sliced. Serve raw in salads with fresh herbs or serve fried, steamed, grilled or baked.

Mooli

This is a root vegetable which belongs to the radish family and is sometimes called white radish or rettiche. It is parsnip shaped but with a smooth white skin. It is bitter in taste rather than hot and contains 24 calories per 100g (4oz). Serve grated in salads, or slice and boil.

Eddoes

Originally from India and Egypt, these potato-like tubers are now grown in West Africa, USA, the West Indies and the South Pacific. Eddoes are root vegetables with a small central bulb surrounded by small tuberous growths covered in a brown hairy skin. They have a white mealy flesh and a potato-like flavour and contain 91 calories per 100g (4oz) cooked and are a good source of vitamin C. Peel and cook as for potatoes.

Green Cauliflower

There are several types of green cauliflower available. Instead of the curds being white they are bright lime green and the flavour is sweeter than that of the white curd variety. They are a good source of vitamin C, especially if served raw. Florets contain 34 calories per 100g (4oz). Green cauliflower cooks quicker than white, but can be used in much the same way.

Thoughts for Everyday

"There is no home that is not twice as beautiful as the most beautiful city."

West African Proverb

"One doesn't discover new lands without consenting to lose sight of the shore for a very long time."

André Gide

"The man who makes no mistakes does not usually make anything."

Edward John Phelps

Name ....

Address ....

....

....

Tel ....

Name ....

Address ....

....

....

Tel ....

Name ....

Address ....

....

....

Tel ....

Name ....

Address ....

....

....

Tel ....

Name ....

Address ....

....

....

Tel ....

O

Custard Apple

Custard apples are native to the West Indies and South America. They are heart-shaped with soft scale-like protruberances, like a pine cone. The skin is green, darkening to patchy brown on ripening. The flesh is creamy white with brown inedible seeds and tastes of custard, cream, vanilla and slightly acidic. To serve, halve, spoon out the flesh and discard the seeds.

Prickly Pear

Also known as Indian Fig, this is a pear shaped cactus fruit. Initially from South America, prickly pears were brought to the Mediterranean by Christopher Columbus, where they are now grown. The skin is greenish orange and covered with sharp prickles. The flesh has a mellow sweet flavour and is pink and juicy with edible seeds. Remove the prickles carefully, peel then slice, and use in fruit salads or purée to use in sauces, ices and jellies.

Mangosteen

A tropical fruit from South East Asia. It has a deep purple fibrous shell about the size of a small apple. Inside the fruit are five creamy white translucent segments each with a seed. The flavour is delicate but fragrant and sweet. Halve and serve in the shell, or remove segments and serve in fruit salads or with sorbets.

Pitabaya

Originating from Central and South America pitahaya is a fruit of the cactus family. It looks like a rubbery yellow grenade; on opening it reveals a mass of tiny black edible seeds. The flavour is quite mild and sweet. Cut in half and scoop out the seeds. Serve in fruit salads or on its own with a dash of lime juice and ground ginger.

Cape Gooseberry/Physalis

A golden berry enclosed in a paper thin husk, these are also known as Chinese lanterns or golden berries and are originally from South America but are now exported from Kenya, India and South Africa. The berry has a delicate lightly scented sharp sweet flavour reminiscent of soft ripe gooseberries. Remove the outer leaves and eat whole or dip into fondant icing to make petit fours.

Pomegranate

Originally from Persia, this has been connected with many cultures and religions. The name derives from Latin and means 'grain apple'. It is an apple-shaped fruit with a tough red and yellow skin with a crown-shaped calyx. On opening it reveals a yellow pith containing translucent red jelly with white seeds. The flesh contains 72 calories per 100g (4oz).

Spoon out the jelly and seeds. Use the fruit in fruit salads or to decorate desserts. To extract the juice, crush the jelly only in a sieve over a bowl and use for jellies and marinades.

Kiwano (Horned Melon, Horned Cucumber)

A bright yellowy orange fruit originally from Kenya, the kiwano is now available from New Zealand. It is ovoid in shape with irregular spikes over the skin. When cut it exposes a green flesh with cucumber like seeds. Cut open and scoop out the flesh and use for fruit salads, with icecream, or as a decoration to desserts.

Limquat

Limquats are closely related to limes and look like small limes. They have a thin rind and pale green flesh. The flavour is similar to a lemon but sharper and more heavily scented. They can be eaten whole including the skin, but are very sharp.

Rambutan

This originates from Malaysia and is sometimes known as a hairy lychee. The red-brown skin is covered with soft hairy dark brown spines and is about 5cm (2 inches) in diameter. The flesh is similar to a lychee for it is pearly white and translucent and contains a large edible brown stone. Peel and serve raw in a light syrup flavoured with ginger or in a fruit salad.

Thoughts for Everyday

"All who joy would win
Must share it, –
Happiness was born a Twin."

Lord Byron: Don Juan

"Everyone complains of
his memory, but no one
complains of his judgement."

La Rochefoucauld

"You can accomplish by
kindness what you cannot
do by force."

Publilius Syrus

Name ....

Address ....

....

....

Tel ....

Name ....

Address ....

....

....

Tel ....

Name ....

Address ....

....

....

Tel ....

Name ....

Address ....

....

....

Tel ....

Name ....

Address ....

....

....

Tel ....

P

COOKING TIMES & METHODS OF SOME VEGETABLES

Vegetable	Steam	Boil	Bake (Whole)	Braise	Stir Fry
Asparagus		10-15 mins			
Beetroot		40-60 mins			
Broad Beans		10-15 mins			
Broccoli	4-8 mins				yes
Brussels Sprouts	6-10 mins		25-30 mins		yes
Cabbage	4-6 mins				yes
Carrots	20 mins	10-15 mins	45-60 mins	15-20 mins	yes
Cauliflower	4-8 mins				
Celery	12-15 mins	8-10 mins		10-12 mins	yes
Chicory					yes
Chinese Leaves	4 mins				yes
Courgettes	4-8 mins				yes
Cucumbers	5-10 mins				
Endive				10-12 mins	
Fennel	12-15 mins	10-12 mins		15-20 mins	yes
French Beans	4-8 mins				yes
Globe Artichokes		30-40 mins			
Jerusalem Artichokes		15-20 mins			
Leeks	15-20 mins	10-15 mins		8-10 mins	
Mangetout Peas	6-8 mins				yes
Marrow	10-12 mins		45-60 mins		yes
Mushrooms					yes
Okra		15-20 mins			
Onions			45-60 mins		
Parsnips		15-20 mins	45-60 mins	15-20 mins	
Peas		8-12 mins			yes
Peppers					yes
Potatoes	25-30 mins	20 mins	1-1½ hours	15-20 mins	
Radish/Daikon					yes
Red Cabbage				45-60 mins	
Swedes	25-30 mins	20 mins		15-20 mins	yes
Sweet Potato	25-30 mins	20 mins	1-1½ hours		
Sweetcorn		8-15 mins			yes
Turnips	25-30 mins	10-15 mins		15-20 mins	yes

These are suggestions only and will give very lightly cooked vegetables. Increase the cooking time for softer vegetables. The freshness of the vegetables may also affect the cooking time.

Thoughts for Everyday

"Hospitality is to be shown
even towards an enemy
The tree doth not withdraw
its shade, even from the
woodcutter."

The Hitopadesa

"Rigid justice is the greatest
injustice."

Thomas Fuller

"You see things and you say,
'Why?' But I dream things
that never were; and I say
'Why not?' "

Thomas Edison

Name ....
Address ....
....
....
Tel ....

Name ....
Address ....
....
....
Tel ....

Name ....
Address ....
....
....
Tel ....

Name ....
Address ....
....
....
Tel ....

Name ....
Address ....
....
....
Tel ....

P

CAKES

Cake mixtures should be of a softer consistency than when baked conventionally. Use an extra tablespoon of milk for each egg added.

STEAMED PUDDINGS

Steamed puddings cook in a fraction of the time of conventional methods, with good results. Serve with custard made in the microwave.

Cake and steamed pudding mixtures rise up more during cooking in a microwave, so use large containers which are no more than half full of raw mixture.

To prevent uncooked mixture on the base of deep cakes or teabreads, stand them on a roasting rack or upturned plate.

MILK

To prevent milk boiling over when cooking soup and sauces, use a container large enough to take twice the amount of liquid.

FISH

Cook fresh fish brushed with milk for succulent flesh. Fresh kippers can be put on a plate with butter on the top and a little vinegar and covered with cling film and cooked on high for 3 mins.

QUICK PORRIDGE

For a quick, nourishing breakfast, serve porridge. Put oats and milk in a bowl and cook on HIGH for 3-4 minutes, stirring occasionally.

SAUCES

Flour-based sauces can be quickly reheated: allow 2-3 minutes on HIGH for 300ml (1/2 pint). Stop and stir occasionally.

GELATINE

Quickly dissolve gelatine by soaking in a measured amount of liquid for a few minutes. Then cook on HIGH for 30-50 seconds. Stop and stir frequently – do not boil.

MILKY DRINK

For a quick milky drink, heat 300ml (1/2 pint) of milk in a mug for approx 2 1/2 minutes on HIGH.

SOFTENING CHEESE

Cheese from the refrigerator can be brought up to room temperature by using DEFROST or LOW power. Allow 2 minutes for 900g (2lb). Butter can also be softened by putting on low for 15/30 secs – WARNING – beware of leaving butter in for too long, it melts very easily from the inside out.

'RIPENING' CHEESE

To 'ripen' semi soft cheeses such as brie place 225g (8oz) on a plate and cook on LOW or DEFROST for 15-45 seconds. Check frequently and leave to stand for 5 minutes before serving. Cook 225g (8oz) soft cheese on HIGH power for 20-30 seconds to soften ready to mix with other ingredients.

CHEESE FONDUE

For a quick cheese fondue, put all the ingredients into a ceramic dish. Allow 7-8 minutes on HIGH for every 450g (lb) of cheese, stirring frequently.

COOKING TIPS

Whether you are cooking from fresh, frozen or thawed state, it is important to turn, stir, rotate and rest foods after cooking to ensure they defrost or cook evenly.

Covering food is often necessary in microwave cooking: it can speed up cooking times, prevent drying out and reduce the splattering of cooking juices on the sides of the oven.

Quick Snacks

SMOKED FISH DIP

(Serves 4)

50g (2 oz) tinned pimento
50g (2 oz) gherkins
80g (3.6 oz) tinned smoked mussels
or oysters, drained
100g (4 oz) fromage frais
1.25ml (1/4 tsp) ginger
lemon juice to taste
sprig of parsley to garnish
crisp biscuits and vegetable sticks to serve

Method
Place the pimento and gherkins in a food processor or liquidiser and process until finely chopped. Add the mussels or oysters and process again until finely chopped. Add the fromage frais and sauce and process until mixed. Spoon into a bowl and chill. Garnish with a sprig of parsley. Serve with crisp biscuits and vegetable sticks

CHEESY AVOCADO TOASTS

(Serves 2)

2 slices wholemeal or granary bread
1/2 ripe avocado
lemon juice
100g (4 oz) cottage cheese
50g (2oz) English Cheddar, grated

Method
Toast one side of each slice of bread. Peel and stone the avocado, dice the flesh and dip in lemon juice. Mix with the cottage cheese and half of the Cheddar cheese. Spoon the mixture onto the untoasted side of the bread, cover with the remaining Cheddar and grill until warm and the Cheddar has melted

CHEESE & GARLIC BREAD

(Makes 2 x 30.5cm (12 inch) loaves)

100g (4oz) butter
3 garlic cloves, skinned and crushed
15ml (1 tbsp) chopped parsley
100g (4 oz) Double Gloucester cheese, grated
2 x 30.5cm (12 inch) loaves

Method
Blend together the butter, garlic and parsley. Stir in the cheese and mix thoroughly.
Make cuts down the loaves at 1 cm intervals almost to the base. Spread the mixture over each side of the bread slices. Wrap the loaves in foil and cook at 200°C (400°F, Gas Mark 6) for 15 minutes, opening up the foil after 10 minutes. Cut into slices and serve.

TARAMASALATA

(Serves 4)

8 oz smoked cod roe
juice of 1 large lemon
6-8 tbsp olive oil
black pepper

Method
Place the roe in a mixing bowl. Add oil and lemon juice alternately, a little at a time, and beat vigorously after each addition until the mixture is a creamy paté. Season to taste with freshly ground black pepper and pack into a dish. Cover and chill lightly. Serve with hot crisp toast, unsalted butter, black olives and lemon wedges.

What Heavenly Smiles!

What heavenly smiles!
  O Lady mine
Through my very heart they shine;
And, if my brow gives back
  their light,
Do thou look gladly on the sight;
As the clear Moon with modest pride
Beholds her own bright beams.
Reflected from the mountain's side
And from the headlong streams.

William Wordsworth

Stolen Pleasure

My sweet did sweetly sleep,
And on her rosy face
Stood tears of pearl, which beauty's
  self did weep;
I, wond'ring at her grace,
Did all amaz'd remain,
When Love said, 'Fool, can looks
  thy wishes crown?
Time past comes not again.'
Then did I me bow down,
And kissing her fair breast, lips,
  cheeks, and eyes,
Prov'd here on earth the joys of
  paradise.

William Drummond of Hawthornden

Name ....
Address ....
....
....
Tel ....

Name ....
Address ....
....
....
Tel ....

Name ....
Address ....
....
....
Tel ....

Name ....
Address ....
....
....
Tel ....

Name ....
Address ....
....
....
Tel ....

Q

Recipe Corner

Starters

BACON & BLUE CHEESE SALAD

(Serves 4)

12 rashers smoked bacon, cut into
*   bite sized pieces*
50g (2 oz) butter
2 garlic cloves crushed
4 thick slices of bread, crusts removed and cut
*   into small squares*
50g (2 oz) Blue Stilton, crumbled
60)ml (4 tbsp) mayonnaise
75ml (3 fl. oz) fresh single cream
black pepper
mixed salad leaves

Method

Cook the bacon in a pan for 7-8 minutes or until crisp and golden. Remove with a slotted spoon and drain on absorbent paper. Add butter to the pan and melt. Add the garlic and bread and cook for 3-4 minutes until crisp and golden. Drain on absorbent paper.

Mix the cheese and mayonnaise together. Stir in the cream and black pepper and beat well to blend.

Mix together the salad leaves, bacon and croutons. Place on serving plates and top with the dressing.

SALMON TROUT & PRAWN PATÉ

(Serves 2)

175g (6oz) sliced smoked salmon trout
50g (2oz) peeled prawns
2.5ml (1/2 tsp) grated lime rind
2.5ml (1/2 tsp) fresh lime juice
freshly ground black pepper
5ml (1 tsp) chopped tarragon
100g (4oz) curd cheese
wedges of lime, prawns to garnish
toast to serve

Method

Line 2 lightly oiled heart shaped moulds or ramekin dishes with half of the salmon trout. Make sure that there is enough fish overlapping the sides to cover the top of the dishes.

Chop the remaining salmon trout and the prawns. Add the lime rind and juice, seasoning, herbs and cheese and mix together well. Divide between the moulds and pack well in. Fold over the overlapping fish to cover the pate.

Chill well before turning out onto serving plates. Garnish with lime wedges and prawns and serve with toast.

FRENCH ONION SOUP

(Serves 4)

2 oz butter or margarine
sliced French bread
2 large onions
grated Gruyère cheese
2 pints of stock
seasoning

Method

Slice the onion thinly and fry in the butter, add the stock and simmer for about 30 minutes. Season with salt and pepper. Meanwhile, sprinkle cheese on the bread slices and brown under a hot grill. Put the bread in bottom of soup bowls and pour the soup on top. Serve immediately.

Thoughts
for
Everyday

"I walk firmer and more
secure uphill than down."

Montaigne

"If a man does not keep pace
with his companions, perhaps it
is because he hears a different
drummer. Let him step to the
music he hears, however
measured or far away."

Thoreau

"He who does not hope to
win has already lost."

José Joaquin Olmedo

Name ....

Address ....

....

....

Tel ....

Name ....

Address ....

....

....

Tel ....

Name ....

Address ....

....

....

Tel ....

Name ....

Address ....

....

....

Tel ....

Name ....

Address ....

....

....

Tel ....

Q

QUICK LIVER PATÉ

(Serves 4)

450g (1lb) chicken livers
25g (1oz) butter
1 medium onion, finely chopped
2 garlic cloves, skinned and crushed
10 drops hot pepper sauce
1.25ml (1/4 tsp) ground bay leaves
2.5ml (1/2 tsp) tomato purée
60ml (4 tbsp) natural yogurt
100g (4oz) curd cheese
30ml (2 tbsp) sherry
sprigs of fresh parsley to garnish

Method
Remove and discard the stringy parts of the livers and roughly chop the remainder. Melt the butter in a non-stick pan, and then add the liver, onion and garlic. Cook until tender, stirring well.
Cool, then place in a blender or food processor with the remaining ingredients. Purée until smooth. Place in a serving dish, cover and chill. Garnish with sprigs of fresh parsley and serve with vegetable sticks and toast.

STUFFED AVOCADOS

(Serves 4)

2 ripe avocados, halved and stoned
juice of 1/2 lemon
100g (4 oz) Stilton, crumbled
75g (3 oz) black seedless grapes, halved
freshly ground black pepper
45ml (3 tbsp) fresh soured cream
25g (1 oz) toasted breadcrumbs

Method
Scoop the flesh from the avocados, chop and mix with the lemon juice. In a bowl mix together the Stilton, grapes, pepper and soured cream with the avocado.
Spoon the mixture back into the avocado shells, and sprinkle the breadcrumbs over the top. Serve with salad.

DEVILLED KIDNEYS

(Serves 2)

350g (12oz) lamb's kidneys, cores removed
25g (1oz) butter
100g (4oz) mushrooms, sliced
15ml (1 tbsp) Worcestershire sauce
30ml (2 tbsp) tomato ketchup
100ml (4 fl oz) fresh whipping cream
cooked rice or toast to serve

Method
Cut the kidneys into bite-sized pieces. Melt the butter in a saucepan, add the kidneys and cook for 2 minutes, stirring well.
Add mushrooms and continue cooking for 3 minutes. Add the sauce, ketchup and cream. Mix well and heat without boiling.
Serve with rice or hot toast and vegetables, sprinkled with chopped parsley.

Thoughts
for
Everyday

"The smallest act of kindness is worth more than the grandest intention."

Author Unidentified

"Experience shows that success is due less to ability than to zeal. The winner is he who gives himself to his work, body and soul."

Charles Buxton

"There is no failure except in no longer trying."

Elbert Hubbard

Name ....

Address ....

....

....

Tel ....

Name ....

Address ....

....

Tel ....

Name ....

Address ....

....

....

Tel ....

Name ....

Address ....

....

....

Tel ....

Name ....

Address ....

....

....

Tel ....

R

CHICKEN & MANGO PLATTER

(Serves 6)

4 boneless skinned chicken breasts
450ml (3/4 pint) chicken stock
200g (7oz) Greek style yogurt
30ml (2 tbsp) mango chutney
5ml (1tsp) curry paste
1/4 head curly endive
large mango, peeled and stoned
1 large avocado
nasturtium flower, to garnish (optional)

Method

Place the chicken breasts in a pan with the stock, bring to the boil, cover and simmer for 30 minutes. Remove from the heat and leave to cool. Cut three of the breasts into slices and chop the remainder.

Mix together the yogurt, mango chutney and curry paste. Place the curly endive on a platter. Slice half the mango and chop the remainder. Peel and stone the avocado, chopping a third of it and slicing the remainder.

Mix together the chopped chicken and mango and add to half of the yogurt mix. Place on a platter. Arrange the chicken, mango and avocado slices on top. Drizzle the remaining yogurt mix over the top and garnish with the flower if desired.

LIVER SPECIAL

(Serves 4)

50g (2oz) flour
2.5ml (1/2 tsp) curry powder
450g (1lb) lamb's liver, cut into strips
50g (2oz) butter
1 onion, sliced
1 green pepper, diced
400ml (14fl oz) fresh milk
200g (7oz) tinned sweetcorn, drained
1 eating apple, peeled, cored and sliced
chopped parsley

Method

Mix the flour and curry powder in a large plastic bag, add the liver and shake to coat with flour. Melt the butter in a large frying pan, add the liver and fry for 3 minutes.

Add the onions and pepper, cook for 3 minutes. Gradually add the milk and bring to the boil, stirring well, until the sauce is thickened.

Add the sweetcorn and apple, and heat through. Serve with mashed potatoes, sprinkled with chopped parsley.

STEAKS WITH STILTON SAUCE

(Serves 2)

2 steaks
15g (1/2oz) butter
1 small onion, finely chopped
30ml (2 tbsp) sherry
100ml (4 fl oz) fresh double cream
15ml (1 tbsp) chopped chives
50g (2oz) Stilton, crumbled
heart shaped toast croutons (optional)

Method

Grill the steaks to your liking

Melt the butter and cook the onion until soft. Stir in the sherry and boil to reduce the liquid slightly. Stir in the cream and chives, heat through, then stir in the Stilton.

Serve the steaks with the sauce, croutons and salad or vegetables.

Thoughts for Everyday

"Experience is a comb which nature gives us when we are bald."

Chinese Proverb

"There are no unimportant jobs, no unimportant people, no unimportant acts of kindness."

Author Unidentified

"Management is the art of getting other people to do the work."

Anon

Name ....
Address ....
....
....
Tel ....

Name ....
Address ....
....
....
Tel ....

Name ....
Address ....
....
....
Tel ....

Name ....
Address ....
....
....
Tel ....

Name ....
Address ....
....
....
Tel ....

R

Main Courses

FAMILY FISH PIE

(Serves 4-6)

50g (2 oz) butter
50g (2 oz) flour
568ml (1 pint) fresh milk
450g (1 lb) smoked haddock, skinned
*   and cubed*
100g (4 oz) frozen peas
200g (7 oz) tinned sweetcorn, drained
2 eggs, hardboiled and chopped
15ml (1 tbsp) chopped parsley
350g (12 oz) potatoes, peeled, diced and cooked
225g (8 oz) swede, peeled, diced and cooked
50g (2 oz) Red Leicester cheese, grated

Method
Place the butter, flour and milk in a saucepan, and bring to the boil, stirring until the sauce thickens and becomes smooth. Add the fish, peas, sweetcorn, egg and parsley and cook for 2-5 minutes. Place in a large ovenproof dish. Keep warm.
Mash the potato and swede with a little extra milk and blend together, then spoon onto the fish mixture, and bake in the oven at a moderate temperature for around 20 minutes.
Sprinkle over the cheese and place under a hot grill for a few minutes until the cheese has melted. Garnish with a sprig of parsley.

TAGLIATELLE ITALIAN STYLE

(Serves 4)

225g (8 oz) tagliatelle
50g (2oz) butter
1 onion, finely chopped
100g (4 oz) button or oyster mushrooms, sliced
100g (4 oz) curd cheese
25g (1 oz) mature English Cheddar, grated
150ml (1/4 pint) fresh single cream
50g (2 oz) smoked or Parma Ham, chopped
25g (1 oz) chopped walnuts
salt and freshly ground black pepper
chopped fresh dill, to garnish

Method
Place the tagliatelle in a large pan of slightly salted boiling water and cook for 7-9 minutes, until just tender or 'al dente'.
Meanwhile heat half the butter in a frying pan, add the onion and cook for 3-4 minutes, until just softened. Add the mushrooms and fry for 2 minutes. Stir in the cheeses, cream, ham, walnuts and seasoning. Lower the heat and simmer for 2-3 minutes.
Drain the pasta, stir in the remaining butter, and season with black pepper. Place on one large or four single serving plates, top with the sauce and serve sprinkled with dill.

Recipe Corner

Main Courses

TUNA & SWEETCORN LASAGNE

(Serves 4)

*400g (14 oz) tinned chopped tomatoes
   with herbs*
1 onion, chopped
50g (2 oz) mushrooms, sliced
1 green pepper seeded and diced
1 garlic clove, peeled and crushed
*400g (14 oz) tinned tuna in brine,
   drained and flaked*
100g (4 oz) tinned sweetcorn, drained
8 sheets of ready-to-cook lasagne
450ml (1/4 pint) fresh milk
75ml (5 tbsp) instant thickening granules
2.5ml (1/2 tsp) mustard
50g (2 oz) mature English Cheddar, grated
pinch of paprika

Method
Fry the garlic and onion together in a little oil
until soft, and then add the tomatoes, pepper
and mushrooms. Cook for another couple of
minutes, then stir in the tuna and sweetcorn and
layer in a 25.5cm x 20.5cm (10 x 8 inch)
ovenproof dish with the lasagne.
Bring the milk to the boil, remove from the heat
and whisk in the thickening granules and stir
until dissolved and the sauce thickens. Add the
mustard and half of the cheese, and pour over
the lasagne. Sprinkle the remaining cheese and
paprika over the top and bake in the oven at
200°C,(400°F, Gas Mark 6) for 35-40 minutes.

FISH CURRY

(Serves 4)

1 onion, chopped
1 garlic clove, skinned and crushed
15g (1/2 oz) butter
30ml (2 tbsp) mild curry powder
450ml (3/4 pint) fresh milk
50g (2 oz) creamed coconut
450g (1lb) white fish fillet, skinned and cubed
1 fish stock cube
100g (4 oz) frozen peas
425g (15 oz) pineapple chunks in natural juice
*227g (8 oz) tinned water chestnuts, drained
   and sliced*
100g (4 oz) peeled prawns
brown rice to serve

Method
Fry the onion and garlic in the butter until soft,
add the curry powder and cook stirring for 1
minute, stirring well.
Gradually blend in the milk, bring to the boil, stir
in the coconut, fish stock cube and peas. Bring
back to the boil, cover and simmer for 5 minutes.
Stir in the remaining ingredients and heat
through. Serve with brown rice.

Twelve Songs, IX

Stop all the clocks, cut off the
* telephone,*
Prevent the dog from barking
* with a juicy bone.*
Silence the pianos and with
* muffled drum*
Bring out the coffin, let the
* mourners come.*

Let aeroplanes circle moaning
* overhead*
Scribbling in the sky the message
* He Is Dead,'*
Put crêpe bows round the white
* necks of the public doves,*
Let traffic policemen wear black
* cotton gloves.*

He was my North, my South,
* my East and West,*
My working week and my
* Sunday rest.*
My noon, my midnight, my talk,
* my song;*
I thought that love would last
* forever: I was wrong.*

The stars are not wanted now:
* put out every one;*
Pack up the moon and dismantle
* the sun;*
Pour away the ocean and sweep
* up the wood.*
For nothing now can ever come
* to any good.*

W H Auden

Name ....

Address ....

....

....

Tel ....

Name ....

Address ....

....

....

Tel ....

Name ....

Address ....

....

....

Tel ....

Name ....

Address ....

....

....

Tel ....

Name ....

Address ....

....

....

Tel ....

S

Recipe Corner

Dessert Recipes

EASY FRUIT BRULÉE

(Serves 4)

350g (12 oz) mixed summer fruits
200ml (7 fl oz) fresh double cream
200g (7 oz) natural yogurt
65g (2 1/2 oz) demerara sugar

Method

Reserve some fruit for decoration. Place the remainder in the base of a flameproof dish. Whip the cream until softly stiff, then fold in the yogurt. Spread over the fruit and chill for 2 hours.

Sprinkle the sugar over the cream and place under a hot grill for a few minutes until the sugar melts and caramelises. Serve hot or cold, decorated with the remaining fruit.

BAKED SOURED CREAM CHEESECAKE

(Serves 10)

50g (2 oz) butter, melted
100g (4 oz) digestive biscuits, crushed
1.25ml (1/4 tsp) ground cinnamon
450g (1lb) cream cheese
150g (5 oz) sugar
3 eggs, beaten
grated rind of 1 lemon
30ml (2 tbsp) lemon juice
7.5ml (1 1/2 tsp) vanilla essence
300ml (10 fl oz) soured cream

Method

Mix together the melted butter, biscuit crumbs and cinnamon. Press into the base of a greased, loose bottomed 20.5cm (8 inch) cake tin. Cook at 180°C (350°F, Gas Mark 4) for 10 minutes.
Beat together the cream cheese and 100g (4 oz) sugar and gradually beat in the eggs. Stir in the lemon rind, juice and 5ml (1tsp) vanilla essence. Pour into the tin and bake for 1 hour or until the

centre is firm to the touch. Remove from the oven and increase to 230°C (450°F, Gas Mark 8). Mix together the remaining ingredients and spread over the cheesecake, bake for 8 minutes, until set. Remove from the oven and cool in the tin to room temperature. Remove the tin and chill until ready to serve. Decorate with lemon and lime rind.

VALENCIA MOUSSE

(Serves 6)

275g (10 oz) plain chocolate,
*   broken into pieces*
5 ml (1 tsp) powdered gelatine
grated rind and juice of 1 orange
4 eggs, separated
25g (1 oz) ground almonds
60ml (1 tbsp) fresh single cream
200ml (7 fl oz) fresh double cream
grated orange zest, to decorate

Method

Place the chocolate in a bowl over a pan of simmering water and heat until melted, stirring occasionally. Sprinkle the gelatine over the orange juice. Place in a pan of hot water and stir until melted.

Remove chocolate from heat, stir in the egg yolks, almonds, single cream, gelatine mix and orange rind. Whip 150 ml (1/4 pint) double cream until it forms soft peaks and fold in. Whisk the egg whites until stiff and fold in. Spoon into 1 large or 6 individual dishes and chill until set. Whip remaining cream and use to decorate mousse. Top with the orange zest and serve.

Thoughts for Everyday

"What I admire in Columbus is not his having discovered a world, but his having gone to search for it on the faith of an opinion."

Author Unidentified

"Life is long to the miserable, but short to the happy."

Publilius Syrus

"Experience is not what happens to you; it is what you do with what happens to you."

Aldous Huxley

Name ....

Address ....

....

....

Tel ....

Name ....

Address ....

....

....

Tel ....

Name ....

Address ....

....

....

Tel ....

Name ....

Address ....

....

....

Tel ....

Name ....

Address ....

....

....

Tel ....

S

Recipe Corner

Vegetarian Recipes

LENTIL LASAGNE

(Serves 4)

15g (1/2 oz) butter
1 medium onion, chopped
1 green pepper, chopped
175g (6 oz) split red lentils
400g (14 oz) tinned tomatoes
300ml (1/2 pint) vegetable stock
300ml (1/2 pint) fresh milk
30ml (2 tbsp) tomato purée
5ml (1 tsp) dried mixed herbs
freshly ground black pepper
8 sheets of ready-to-cook lasagne
2 eggs
225g (8 oz) natural yogurt
100g (4 oz) English Cheddar, grated

Method

Melt the butter in a saucepan, add the onion and cook until soft. Add the peppers lentils, tomatoes, stock 150ml (1/4 pint) milk, tomato puree, herbs and pepper.

Bring to the boil, cover and simmer for 15-20 minutes until the lentils are tender. Place half of the lentil mixture in the base of a 25.5 x 20.5cm (10 x 8 inch) ovenproof dish, cover with half of the lasagne, repeat the layers.

Whisk together the eggs, remaining milk and yogurt. Stir in half of the cheese and pour over the lasagne. Sprinkle the remaining cheese over the lasagne and bake at 220°C (400°F, Gas Mark 6) for 35-40 minutes or until golden brown.

VEGETABLE CRUNCH

Serves 4

75g (3 oz) butter
1 onion, sliced
30ml (2 tbsp) tomato purée
225g (8 oz) broccoli florets
225g (8 oz) carrots, sliced
175g (6 oz) mushrooms, sliced
397g (14 oz) tinned chopped tomatoes
15ml (1 tbsp) fresh chopped parsley
2.5ml (1/2 tsp) mixed dried herbs
100g (4 oz) unsalted nuts
75g (3 oz) wholemeal flour
25g (1 oz) rolled oats
100g (4 oz) vegetarian Cheddar, grated
fresh coriander to garnish

Method

Melt 25g (1 oz) of butter in a pan, add the onions and tomato puree and cook until onions are soft. Add remaining vegetables and herbs. Fry gently for 10 minutes until the vegetables are cooked. Add the nuts and place in an ovenproof dish and allow to cool.

Rub the remaining butter into the flour until it resembles fine breadcrumbs then stir in the rolled oats and most of the cheese.

Spoon over the crumble mixture, and sprinkle with the remaining cheese.

Bake at 200°C (400°F, Gas Mark 6) for 30 minutes until browned. Garnish with coriander.

Thoughts for Everyday

"Laughter has no foreign accent."

Paul Lowney

"To be capable of steady friendship or lasting love, are the two greatest proofs, not only of goodness of heart, but of strength of mind."

William Hazlitt

"The only thing we have to fear is fear itself."

F D Roosevelt

Name ....
Address ....
....
....
Tel ....

Name ....
Address ....
....
....
Tel ....

Name ....
Address ....
....
....
Tel ....

Name ....
Address ....
....
....
Tel ....

Name ....
Address ....
....
....
Tel ....

T

Dinner Party Records

Date/Occasion ....

Guests

Menu/Notes

Date/Occasion ....

Guests

Menu/Notes

Date/Occasion ....

Guests

Menu/Notes

Date/Occasion ....

Guests

Menu/Notes

Thoughts
for
Everyday

"Don't carry a grudge.
While you're carrying the
grudge the other guy's
out dancing."

Buddy Hackett

"I never did anything worth
doing by accident, nor did
any of my inventions come by
accident; they came by work."

Thomas A Edison

"Sports do not build
character. They reveal it."

Heywood Broun

Name ....

Address ....

....

....

Tel ....

Name ....

Address ....

....

....

Tel ....

Name ....

Address ....

....

....

Tel ....

Name ....

Address ....

....

....

Tel ....

Name ....

Address ....

....

....

Tel ....

T

Dinner Party Records

Date/Occasion ....

Guests   Menu/Notes

Date/Occasion ....

Guests   Menu/Notes

Date/Occasion ....

Guests   Menu/Notes

Date/Occasion ....

Guests   Menu/Notes

Dinner Party Records

Date/Occasion ....

Guests

Menu/Notes

....

....

....

....

....

Date/Occasion ....

Guests

Menu/Notes

....

....

....

....

....

Food Preferences

Little can be so disheartening to the cook to learn that a meal that has been hours in the preparation is poison to one of the guests - maybe he or she is a vegetarian, allergic to eggs, detests olives . . . !
Avoid uncomfortable situations by keeping a record of your friends' most important food preferences.

Friend ....   Friend ....

Allergies/ ....   Allergies/ ....

Dislikes ....   Dislikes ....

Friend ....   Friend ....

Allergies/ ....   Allergies/ ....

Dislikes ....   Dislikes ....

Friend ....   Friend ....

Allergies/ ....   Allergies/ ....

Dislikes ....   Dislikes ....

Friend ....   Friend ....

Allergies/ ....   Allergies/ ....

Dislikes ....   Dislikes ....

Love's Memories

Love's memories haunt my
　　footsteps still
Like ceaseless flowings of the river.
Its mystic depths say what can fill?
Sad disappointment waits forever.

John Clare

The Defiance

By Heaven 'tis false, I am not vain;
And rather would the subject be
Of your indifference, or disdain,
Than wit or raillery.

Take back the trifling praise you
　　give,
And pass it on some other fool,
Who may the injuring wit believe,
That turns her into ridicule.

Tell her, she's witty, fair, and gay,
With all the charms that can
　　subdue:
Perhaps she'll credit what you say;
But curse me if I do.

If your diversion you design,
On my good-nature you have
　　prest:
Or if you do intend it mine,
You have mistook the jest.

Aphra Behn

Name ....
Address ....
....
....
Tel ....

Name ....
Address ....
....
....
Tel ....

Name ....
Address ....
....
....
Tel ....

Name ....
Address ....
....
....
Tel ....

Name ....
Address ....
....
....
Tel ....

U

Family History

Use these pages to keep a record of your immediate family history

HUSBAND'S GENEALOGY

Husband's Full Name ....

Birth Date ....

Birth Place ....

Special Comments ....

....

....

....

The Marriage

_____

and

_____

were joined together in marriage on

_____

at

_____

WIFE'S GENEALOGY

Wife's Full Name ....

Birth Date ....

Birth Place ....

Special Comments ....

....

....

....

"To forget one's ancestors is to be a brook without a source, a tree without a root."
Chinese Proverb

Thoughts for Everyday

"The only place where success comes before work is in a dictionary."

Vidal Sassoon

"There is always time to add a word, never to withdraw one."

Baltasar Gracián

"Do not use a hatchet to remove a fly from your friend's forehead."

Chinese Proverb

Name ....
Address ....
....
....
Tel ....

Name ....
Address ....
....
....
Tel ....

Name ....
Address ....
....
....
Tel ....

Name ....
Address ....
....
....
Tel ....

Name ....
Address ....
....
....
Tel ....

U

Family History

Parents

Husband's Father

Date of
Marriage

Other Children

Husband

Husband's Mother

Date of
Marriage

Wife's Father

Date of
Marriage

Wife

Other Children

Wife's Mother

Thoughts for Everyday

"I can resist everything except temptation."

Oscar Wilde

"Change is the law of life. And those who look only to the past or the present are certain to miss the future."

John F Kennedy

"I'd like to be rich enough so I could throw soap away after the letters are worn off."

Andy Rooney

Name ....

Address ....

....

....

Tel ....

Name ....

Address ....

....

....

Tel ....

Name ....

Address ....

....

....

Tel ....

Name ....

Address ....

....

....

Tel ....

Name ....

Address ....

....

....

Tel ....

V

Family History

OUR ANCESTORS

Grandparents | Great Grandparents

Husband's Father

Husband's Paternal Grandfather's Name
- Husband's Great Grandfather's Name
- Husband's Great Grandmother's Name

Husband's Paternal Grandmother's Name
- Husband's Great Grandfather's Name
- Husband's Great Grandmother's Name

Husband's Mother

Husband's Maternal Grandfather's Name
- Husband's Great Grandfather's Name
- Husband's Great Grandmother's Name

Husband's Maternal Grandmother's Name
- Husband's Great Grandfather's Name
- Husband's Great Grandmother's Name

Wife's Mother

Wife's Paternal Grandfather's Name
- Wife's Great Grandfather's Name
- Wife's Great Grandmother's Name

Wife's Paternal Grandmother's Name
- Wife's Great Grandfather's Name
- Wife's Great Grandmother's Name

Wife's Father

Wife's Maternal Grandfather's Name
- Wife's Great Grandfather's Name
- Wife's Great Grandmother's Name

Wife's Maternal Grandmother's Name
- Wife's Great Grandfather's Name
- Wife's Great Grandmother's Name

Thoughts for Everyday

"When spiders' webs unite, they can tie up a lion."

Ethiopian Proverb

"In heaven above, and earth below, they best can serve true gladness who meet most feelingly the calls of sadness."

William Wordsworth

"We must all hang together, or assuredly we shall all hang separately."

Benjamin Franklin

Name ....

Address ....

....

....

Tel ....

Name ....

Address ....

....

....

Tel ....

Name ....

Address ....

....

....

Tel ....

Name ....

Address ....

....

....

Tel ....

Name ....

Address ....

....

....

Tel ....

W

OUR DESCENDENTS

Our Children

Our Grand-Children

Born

Spouse

Born

Spouse

Born

Spouse

Born

Spouse

Born

Spouse

Born

Spouse

Husband

Wife

Family History

Use this page to record any special details about your family – the history of the family name, famous people in your lineage, family traits . . .

To Celia

Drink to me, only, with thine eyes,
And I will pledge with mine;
Or leave a kiss but in the cup
And I'll not look for wine.
The thirst that from the soul
    doth rise
Doth ask a drink divine;
But might I of Jove's nectar sup
I would not change for thine.

I sent thee late a rosy wreath,
Not so much honouring thee
As giving it a hope, that there
It could not wither'd be;
But thou thereon did;st only breath
And sent'st it back to me;
Since when it grows, and smells,
    I swear,
Not of itself, but thee.

Ben Jonson

from The Anniversary

All other things to their destruction
    draw,
Only our love hath no decay;
This, no tomorrow hath, nor
    yesterday,
Running it never runs from us
    away,
But truly keeps his first, last,
    everlasting day.

John Donne

Name ....

Address ....

....

....

Tel ....

Name ....

Address ....

....

....

Tel ....

Name ....

Address ....

....

....

Tel ....

Name ....

Address ....

....

....

Tel ....

Name ....

Address ....

....

....

Tel ....

W

Thoughts for Everyday

"When brothers agree, no fortress is so strong as their common life."

Antisthenes

"Courage is resistance to fear, mastery of fear, not absence of fear."

Mark Twain

"The only solid and lasting peace between a man and his wife is, doubtless, a separation."

Lord Chesterfield

Name ....

Address ....

....

....

Tel ....

Name ....

Address ....

....

....

Tel ....

Name ....

Address ....

....

....

Tel ....

Name ....

Address ....

....

....

Tel ....

Name ....

Address ....

....

....

Tel ....

X

Thoughts for Everyday

"Don't be afraid to take big steps. You can't cross a chasm in two small jumps."

David Lloyd George

"The art of dining well is no slight art, the pleasure not a slight pleasure."

Montaigne

"I guess walking slow getting married is because it gives you time to maybe change your mind."

Virginia Cary Hudson

Name ....
Address ....
....
....
Tel ....

Name ....
Address ....
....
....
Tel ....

Name ....
Address ....
....
....
Tel ....

Name ....
Address ....
....
....
Tel ....

Name ....
Address ....
....
....
Tel ....

Y

Thoughts for Everyday

"A man's real possession is his memory. In nothing else is he rich, in nothing else is he poor."

Alexander Smith

"He who has gone, so we but cherish his memory, abides with us, more potent, nay, more present, than the living man."

Saint Exupéry

"Always be a little kinder than necessary."

James M Barrie

Name ....

Address ....

....

....

Tel ....

Name ....

Address ....

....

....

Tel ....

Name ....

Address ....

....

....

Tel ....

Name ....

Address ....

....

....

Tel ....

Name ....

Address ....

....

....

Tel ....

Z